DISCOVERING LANGUAGES
SPANISH

TEACHER'S EDITION

Elaine S. Robbins

Formerly Mount Logan Middle School
Logan, Utah

Kathryn R. Ashworth

Brigham Young University

Dedicated to serving

AMSCO

our nation's youth

AMSCO SCHOOL PUBLICATIONS, INC.
315 Hudson Street / New York, N.Y. 10013

Cassettes

The DISCOVERING LANGUAGES series includes one cassette for each language, except Latin. The voices are those of native speakers.

Each cassette includes the following material:

Oral exercises in four-phased sequences: cue—pause for student response—correct response by native speaker—pause for student repetition.

The dialogs at normal listening speed.

Questions or completions in four-phased sequences.

Seven or eight songs for each language, sung with guitar accompaniment.

The Spanish cassette (Ordering Code N 594 C) is available separately from the publisher. A complete cassette script is included.

When ordering this book, please specify R 594 T or DISCOVERING LANGUAGES: SPANISH, TEACHER'S EDITION

ISBN 0-87720-138-2

Copyright © 1995 by Amsco School Publications, Inc.

Songs written by Rupert Johnson.

Printed in the United States of America

1 2 3 4 5 6 7 8 9 10   02 01 00 99 98 97 96 95 94

Preface

DISCOVERING LANGUAGES is a four-color foreign language program consisting of five separate texts: French, German, Italian, Spanish, and Latin. An additional component, *Origins and History of Language,* suitable for reproduction, is an integral part of the program and is included in this Teacher's Edition. DISCOVERING LANGUAGES is designed for either a one-year or one-semester course in upper-elementary or middle-school Foreign Language Exploratory programs, commonly known as FLEX. The DISCOVERING LANGUAGES Program aims to:

➡ Offer students an opportunity to begin communicating in different foreign languages in a formal course before choosing one language for further study.

➡ Foster a global perspective by exposing students to several foreign languages, the countries where they are spoken, and the people who speak them.

➡ Heighten students' appreciation and respect for cultural diversity and sharpen their cross-cultural awareness and sensitivity.

➡ Introduce students to the rich ethnic heritage of the English language and provide them with an insight into the nature of language, its origins and early development, language families, and similarities among languages.

➡ Develop interdisciplinary skills by linking foreign language study with language arts, social studies, and math.

DISCOVERING LANGUAGES is designed to give students the opportunity to begin communicating in a foreign language in a natural, personalized, enjoyable, and rewarding context. Communication is developed through simple materials in visually focused topical contexts.

The text for each language of the DISCOVERING LANGUAGES Program includes an introduction to the specific country, its language and people. A final review section practices and reinforces the vocabulary and culture taught in preceding sections. Illustrated cultural notes offer views and insights into aspects of foreign life that students can easily relate to their own lives.

Each section includes a variety of activities designed to give students the feeling that not only can they learn all that has been presented but that they can also have fun practicing the foreign language. Activities include dialogs in cartoon-strip fashion, picture-cued exercises and puzzles, skits and conversations, coloring activities, songs, and games. The words and expressions, as well as the language structures introduced in DISCOVERING LANGUAGES, have been carefully chosen and limited to insure student comfort and success.

Origins and History of Language

A sixteen-page discussion on the origins and history of language, suitable for reproduction, is included in each Teacher's Edition. It covers prehistoric messages, early systems of writing, early alphabets, languages of Europe; a history of the English language, the Latin-English connection, and information on the richness of language of American place-names. An integral component of DISCOVERING LANGUAGES, this unit provides an interesting introduction to the program.

Vocabulary

Each section begins with topically related illustrations that convey the meanings of new words in the target language without recourse to English. This device enables students to make a direct and vivid association between the foreign terms and their meanings. Most activities use illustrations and picture cues to practice words and expressions.

To facilitate comprehension an early section of each book is devoted to cognates of English words. Beginning a course in this way shows students that the target language is not so "foreign" after all and helps them overcome any fears they may have about the difficulty of learning a language. Words and expressions are limited and structure is simple and straightforward. Because students are not overburdened, they quickly gain a feeling of success.

Conversation

Students learn to express themselves and talk about their families and friends. They learn to greet people, to tell the day and month of the year, to identify and describe people and objects, and more. Skits and conversational activities follow situational dialogs in cartoon-strip style, encouraging students to begin using the target language for communication and self-expression. These activities serve as a springboard for personalized communication in pairs or groups.

Pronunciation

Throughout each book of the series, a lively and often humorous cartoon detective will guide students on how to pronounce the sounds and words of the particular language.

Songs

Each language component, except Latin, includes seven or eight songs in its Teacher's Edition, incorporating much of the vocabulary of the book and providing an amusing and effective learning tool. The songs include numbers, days of the week, colors, parts of the body, and more. Musical arrangements and lyrics, as well as English translations, are provided in the Teacher's Editions and the cassette scripts.

Culture

The first section of each book introduces students to the foreign language, its speakers, and the countries where it is spoken. Illustrated cultural notes follow most sections and offer students a variety of views and insights into well-known and not so well-known aspects of the culture: school, holidays, leisure time, sports, and interesting manners and customs.

Teacher's Editions

The Teacher's Edition for each language provides a wealth of suggestions and strategies for teaching all elements in the book. Also included are supplementary listening and speaking activities, total physical response activities, projects and research topics, and additional cultural information to supplement the cultural notes in the student book. The Teacher's Editions also include musical arrangements and lyrics for the target language songs together with English translations for the songs and a complete Key to all exercises and puzzles.

Cassettes

A cassette with a printed script is available from the publisher for each language except Latin. It includes oral exercises, questions, completions, and dialogs, all with appropriate pauses for response or repetition. The cassettes also include the songs in the Teacher's Editions, sung with guitar accompaniment.

Teacher Preparation

The DISCOVERING LANGUAGES Program is designed with the foreign-language teacher as well as the non-foreign-language teacher in mind. The simple and straightforward vocabulary and structures taught in the course can be easily mastered by teachers with little knowledge of the target language. Instructors with no knowledge of the foreign language will find the Teacher's Edition and the cassette accompanying each language component particularly useful tools.

Origins and History of Language

I Prehistoric Messages

About one hundred years ago, river pebbles were discovered under layers of debris in a cave in southern France. These pebbles, untouched for tens of thousands of years, were decorated with lines and dots of a red paint called ocher. The markings resembled a form of writing. What was the purpose of these marked pebbles? Scientists guessed that they were good-luck charms, but no one knew with certainty.

In the early 1960s, the scientist Alexander Marshack discovered prehistoric bones gouged with scratches and marks. He explained these markings as examples of early people's efforts to count, tally, and number objects. Many similar bones have been found since that time.

As early as thirty thousand years ago, cave dwellers in Spain and France told stories about hunting by painting pictures on cave walls. These picture stories are the earliest known examples of "written" ideas. A cave in Altamira, Spain, contains some of the most important examples of cave art. The pictures at Altamira show bisons, wild horses, deer with huge antlers, and strange prehistoric creatures in yellow, red, brown, and black. What inspired these pictures? What was their purpose? Some have guessed that primitive people painted these scenes to bring them luck in the hunt.

For thousands of years, people expressed themselves by drawing, painting, and etching on rocks and other surfaces. Storytelling pictures in caves have been discovered in many areas of the world. From them we have learned much about how prehistoric people built huts, plowed, planted, and performed a variety of other activities. They give us a glimpse into the life and customs of prehistoric people.

Stone markings, cave paintings, and bone decorations are the earliest forms of "written" communication. Although spoken language came before written language, we do not know how prehistoric people spoke. Did they communicate by making animal sounds? For example, did they refer to a cat by making the sound *meow*, and did *meow* then become the word for cat? These and many other questions may never be answered.

Activity A

1. Where and when were pebbles with primitive markings resembling writing discovered?

_____

2. What did the markings mean?

_____

3. Which came first, speaking or writing?

_____

4. How many years ago were animals painted in the cave in Altamira, Spain?

_____

5. What can we learn from cave art?

_____

2 Early Systems of Writing

Over many thousands of years, people invented and discovered ways to improve their lives. They learned to raise crops by using irrigation; they learned to weave cloth, to build houses, chariots, ships with sails; and they developed tools and weapons. They began to live in cities and trade the goods they produced. As life grew more and more complex, it became essential to find a way to record and communicate the ever-increasing amount of information people had to remember. And so people began to write.

The earliest people to develop a form of writing were the Sumerians, who lived in an ancient land called Mesopotamia, known today as Iraq, about five thousand years ago.

The Sumerians advanced far beyond their neighbors because their efficient method of writing replaced complicated pictures or scratches on bones. At first the Sumerians created a system of writing made up of many simplified pictures that stood for words. For example, a crown would mean king, a spear would mean kill, waves would mean sea, and so on. The next step the Sumerians took to make their writing less complicated is the single most important step in the history of writing. To make it easier to understand this important step, let's pretend that the Sumerians spoke English.

At the beginning, Sumerians used one picture for every word in their language. To write the word *sea*—the body of water—they used one picture, ∿∿∿, and to write the verb *to see* they used another picture, 👁 👁 . At a certain point, the Sumerians realized that two different pictures were not necessary to express the same-sounding word. So they began to use one picture for both words. For example, they chose this picture, ∿∿∿ , to write both the words *sea* and *to see*.

With time, they went one step further. They began to use the picture ∿∿∿

whenever the sound *see* occurred WITHIN a word. For the word *season*, for example, they used the symbol ∿∿∿ followed by the symbol for *sun* and wrote *season* like this: ∿∿∿ + ○ .

If we wrote English using the Sumerian way of writing, this is how we would write the following words:

kitten

starfish

And these sentences would be written as follows:

Aunt saw king.

King told seaman to sail.

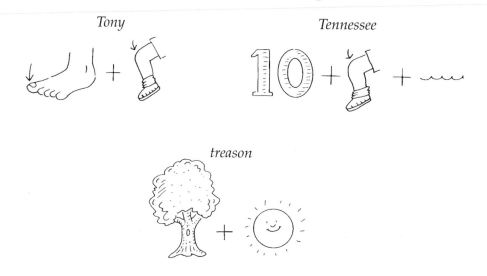

Having picture symbols stand for sounds not only cut down on the thousands of pictures the Sumerians needed to remember but also made it possible to write words that could not be illustrated with a picture, such as names of people, cities, and abstract words. Here are some examples:

Tony

Tennessee

treason

Does this remind you of a game? You have probably played the rebus game. That is exactly how writing began.

Activity B

Now you try. Write the following words using the rebus principle:

1. penmanship _____

2. horseshoe _____

3. many _____

4. penny _____

5. seesaw _____

6. skinny _____

7. heartless _____

8. heartburn _____

9. tighten _____

10. timeless _____

11. cowboy _____

12. kitten _____

3 Early Alphabets

In order to write in ancient Sumerian, hundreds of symbols had to be memorized and the symbols had to be carefully written. Since it was difficult for everyone to learn so many symbols, writing became the job of a small number of people called scribes. In time, scribes improved and simplified the symbols of the written language in order to make their work easier.

It took the Sumerians a long time to come up with an efficient and accurate writing system known as cuneiform. The Sumerians pressed their writing instruments into clay tablets while the clay was damp and soft. Some of their neighbors—the Babylonians, the Assyrians, and the Persians—borrowed the idea of writing from the Sumerians and adapted it to the sounds of their own languages.

The ancient Egyptians developed a different writing system. Like the Sumerians, they also used symbols and signs that stood for words and parts of words, but they created symbols called hieroglyphs. They wrote on papyrus scrolls instead of clay tablets. Papyrus was a paperlike material made from the fibers of reeds that grew along the Nile River.

The next important step in the history of writing was taken by the Phoenicians, who lived along the easternmost coast of the Mediterranean Sea. They realized the value of writing but found the picture writing of the Egyptians complicated and awkward. Instead, the Phoenicians developed a system of only 22 to 30 symbols. This system was not like the Sumerian and Egyptian writing systems where a picture symbol stood for a whole word or part of a word. In the Phoenician writing system, one symbol stood for a single consonant plus a vowel sound.

The alphabet was the next step. When the Greeks started using separate symbols for vowels and consonants, the first true alphabet was created.

The alphabet developed by the Greeks was to become the foundation of the Roman alphabet, which is very similar to the one we use today. The Greeks also gave us the word *alphabet*. *Alpha* is the first letter of the Greek alphabet, and *beta* is the second.

Now compare the different writing systems illustrated on page *xiii*. Note that the Egyptian symbols date back to 3000 B.C., the Phoenician symbols to 1000 B.C., the Greek alphabet to 600 B.C., and the Roman alphabet to A.D. 114. Capital letters were the only forms used in the Greek and Roman alphabets. Lowercase letters developed gradually from the small letters used by scribes who needed to fit more words in the books they copied by hand.

The Roman alphabet closely resembles our modern alphabet except for the letters *J, U,* and *W,* which were added to the alphabet during the Middle Ages.

Egyptian	Phoenician	Greek	Roman
𓂝	ⱄ	Λ	A
⌐	⟨	B	B
⟩	⟨	Γ	C
◻	△	△	D
𓀠	⟨	E	E
Y	Y	F	F
⟩	⟨	Γ	G
⌂	⟨	A	H
⌐	⟨	I	I
⌐	⟨	I	I
⌐	↓	K	K
⟍	⟨	∧	L
⁓⁓⁓	ⱄ	M	M

Egyptian	Phoenician	Greek	Roman
𓆙	ⱄ	N	N
👁	O	O	O
⊂⊃	⟨	Γ	P
𓇟	Φ	G	Q
𓁶	⟨	P	R
⌣	W	Σ	S
×	+	T	T
Y	Y	Υ	V
Y	Y	Υ	V
Y	Y	Υ	V
	‡	X	X
Y	Y	Υ	Y
𓂋	I	Z	Z

Activity C

1. Who were the people who made cuneiform writings on clay tablets?

_____

2. What was the name of the land where these people lived?

_____

3. Why did the Sumerians need to invent writing?

_____

4. Did every Sumerian learn cuneiform writing? Why or why not?

_____

5. What was the writing of the ancient Egyptians called?

_____

6. How was Phoenician writing different from hieroglyphics and cuneiform writing?

_____

7. What was the name of the people who invented the first true alphabet?

_____

8. Where does the word _alphabet_ come from?

_____

4 The Languages of Europe

About three thousand languages are spoken around the world. All these languages have been grouped into nine major families. Language families are groups of languages that are related because they developed from a single common language called the parent language.

Indo-European is the most widespread language family in the world. About half of the world's population today speaks an Indo-European language, including most of the people of modern Europe. All the Indo-European languages came from the same parent language. Although there are no records of the parent language, scientists believe that a very long time ago speakers of this language lived in central Europe. As these people grew in number, they moved into other areas of the European continent and of the world. Some went to the country we now call Greece. Others went to Italy, France, and England. Some moved north to the Baltic countries, and still others went east to Russia. The farthest any of these people are believed to have gone is Asia Minor and northern India.

These groups took their language with them, but once they were separated from one another, the parent language they all spoke began to change. Now, after thousands of years, the language of each group has changed so much that one group cannot understand the other.

The Indo-European family of languages is divided into several smaller groups or subgroups. The following is a partial list of these subgroups and the modern languages that evolved from them:

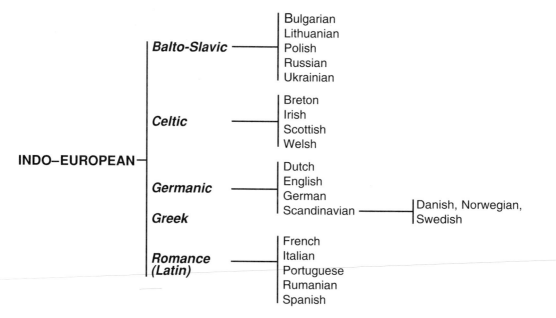

INDO–EUROPEAN

Balto-Slavic
- Bulgarian
- Lithuanian
- Polish
- Russian
- Ukrainian

Celtic
- Breton
- Irish
- Scottish
- Welsh

Germanic
- Dutch
- English
- German
- Scandinavian — Danish, Norwegian, Swedish

Greek

Romance (Latin)
- French
- Italian
- Portuguese
- Rumanian
- Spanish

Activity D

Now, with your teacher's help, look at a world map and identify those countries whose languages belong to the Indo-European family of languages.

Although the sounds and forms of the original Indo-European parent language have changed, many of its basic words are still found in different modern languages today.

Look at the similarities in these examples:

ENGLISH	LATIN	ITALIAN	FRENCH	SPANISH	GERMAN
circus	circus	circo	cirque	circo	Zirkus
mother	mater	madre	mère	madre	Mutter
nature	natura	natura	nature	naturaleza	Natur
nose	nasus	naso	nez	nariz	Nase
stadium	stadium	stadio	stade	estadio	Stadion

English derived from the Germanic subgroup, but it also contains many words of the Romance subgroup of languages.

The three most widely spoken languages of the Western Hemisphere are English, Spanish, and Portuguese. French, another European language, is also spoken by several million people in eastern Canada and the Caribbean. English, Spanish, Portuguese, and French explorers and settlers were the first Europeans to bring their languages to the New World.

Languages are always changing. As we speak, new words are being created and added to our own English language. Every new discovery in science and technology, for example, requires a new word. Think about it. Did the words *laser* and *compact disc* exist fifty years ago?

New words are also added to English when words are borrowed from other languages. In English, for example, we use the German words **gesundheit** and **pumpernickel,** the French words **ballet** and **boutique,** the Italian words **maestro** and **fiasco,** and the Spanish words **pimiento** and **patio.**

Activity E

1. Name the three leading languages of the Western Hemisphere.

_____

2. Name a fourth European language that is spoken in eastern Canada.

_____

3. What is the name of the language family from which scientists think most European languages came?

_____

4. Name five modern languages of the Romance language subgroup.

_____

5. English is a combination of which two language subgroups?

_____

6. Name five words that have been created and added to English in the last fifty years.

_____

7. Name five foreign words that English has borrowed from other languages.

_____

5 History of the English Language

English is the most widely spoken language in the world today. The origins of the English language go way back to a language spoken more than two thousand years ago by people called the Celts, who lived in what is now England.

The history of the English language can be divided into three periods:

1. The Old English period, from 500 to 1000
2. The Middle English period, from 1100 to 1500
3. The Modern English period, from 1500 to the present

During this long span of time, England was invaded and ruled by people from different areas of Europe, each bringing with them their own languages.

First came the Romans who conquered England and ruled over the Celts from 50 B.C. to A.D. 400. Around A.D. 450, three Germanic tribes known as the Jutes, the Angles, and the Saxons invaded England. These tribes brought with them Germanic languages that resemble modern German. With time these languages mixed to form what is called Old English, also known as Anglo-Saxon.

During the mid-1000s, the Normans, a people living in northern France, invaded England. They brought with them the French language of the time. The people of England borrowed thousands of French words and made them part of their own language. The pronunciation and word order of Old English also changed under the influence of the Normans.

In addition to French, a great number of Latin words entered the language spoken in England. Latin was an influential language used by church officials and courts of law. The language that resulted from the mixture of Old English, French, and Latin is called Middle English.

By the sixteenth century, Middle English had changed so much that a person who spoke Old English would not have understood it. Over the next few hundred years, English borrowed words from many different languages and slowly developed into Modern English.

Beginning in the 1600s, the English language began to spread across the world as the English explored and colonized North America, Africa, Australia, and India.

6 The Latin-English Connection

More than half of all English words come from Latin. Some English words are spelled exactly like Latin: **odor, color, circus.** In many other words, the only difference between English and Latin is one or two letters: **machina, natura, familia.**

Here is a list of Latin words and their meanings. Now look at the English word that comes from the Latin word. Write the definition of each of the English words in the empty boxes.

LATIN	MEANING	ENGLISH	DEFINITION
agricola	*farmer*	agriculture	
canis	*dog*	canine	
digitus	*finger*	digit	
femina	*woman*	feminine	
lavare	*to wash*	lavatory	
salutare	*to greet*	salute	
venditare	*to sell*	vendor	
laborare	*to work*	laboratory	

Now look at these Latin words and their meanings. Find an English word that comes from the Latin. You may be able to come up with more than one English word. An example is given to get you started.

LATIN	MEANING	ENGLISH WORD(S)
pes	*foot*	pedal, pedicure, pedestrian
aqua	*water*	
dentes	*teeth*	
libri	*books*	
frigidus	*cold*	
vocabulum	*word*	
spectare	*to watch*	
portare	*to carry*	
lavare	*to wash*	
computare	*to count, do figures*	

Many other English words are often made up of two Latin words. For example, the English word *submarine* comes from the Latin prefix **sub-** meaning "under" and the Latin root (or base) **marinus** meaning "sea." The short Latin word **sub-** is called a prefix because it is placed before the root. Look at how it works:

PREFIX	+	ROOT	=	LITERAL ENGLISH MEANING	ENGLISH WORD
sub-	+	**marinus**	=	*under the sea*	*submarine*

Now you do it. Here is a list of common prefixes + root words and their meanings. Can you combine them to form English words? Write the literal English meaning and the English word in the empty boxes. Some examples are given to get you started.

PREFIX	+	ROOT	=	LITERAL ENGLISH MEANING	ENGLISH WORD
in- *in, into*	+	**vadere** *to advance*	=	*to advance into*	*invade*
circum- *around*	+	**navigare** *to sail*	=	*to sail around*	*circumnavigate*
ex- *out of, from*	+	**portare** *to carry*	=		
im- *in, into*	+	**portare** *to carry*	=		
trans- *across*	+	**portare** *to carry*	=		
in- *in, into*	+	**habitare** *to live*	=		
intro- *in, inward*	+	**ducere** *to lead*	=		
inter- *between*	+	**rumpere** *to break*	=		
sub- *under*	+	**terrenus** *earth*	=		
suc- *up*	+	**cedere** *to go*	=		
pro *forward*	+	**cedere** *to go*	=		

As you can see, the Latin-English connection is a strong one. If we took a closer look at German, as well as other European languages, we would also find thousands of words that resemble English. By learning a foreign language not only are we able to communicate with and appreciate people from different countries and cultures, we also learn a lot about our own language, English.

7 Language Richness of American Place-Names

Spanish Place-Names

The Spanish language first came to America in 1492 with Christopher Columbus's expedition. In the following years, Spanish spread across the lands conquered and settled by Spanish explorers.

Many names of American cities, especially in the West, come from Spanish. Las Vegas (Nevada) means "the meadows"; Sacramento (California) means "sacrament"; Pueblo (Colorado) means "town"; and Los Angeles (California) means "the angels." San Francisco is Spanish for "Saint Francis," and San Diego for "Saint James."

There are Spanish place-names for states as well. Florida was originally called **Pascua Florida,** Spanish for "flowered Easter." Montana means "mountain." Colorado comes from the Spanish word **colorado** meaning "colored" or "reddish," the color of the Colorado River when it carries a load of silt through the red rock country it crosses.

Many other Spanish place-names are found in the East, West, and Southwest. The mountain range between Nevada and California is called the Sierra Nevada, Spanish for "snowy mountain range." The Alamo in Texas is Spanish for "poplar tree," a tree that grew where settlers found water.

Native American Place-Names

Native Americans lived in North America before the Spanish, English, or French settled in America. The Mohawks, Oneidas, Onondagas, Cayugas, and Senecas made up the five Iroquois nations of central New York. Many American Indian words remain for states, cities, mountains, and rivers in that area and across the United States. Lakes Michigan, Huron, and Erie, as well as the Mississippi and Missouri rivers, come from Indian names. These names were also given to cities and states. Other state names that came from the Indians are Illinois, Massachusetts, Minnesota, Alaska, Connecticut, and Utah.

English Place-Names

The East Coast of the United States was colonized by the English, and many of its place-names are of English origin. The Puritans who sailed on the *Mayflower* named Plymouth after an English city. The cities of Boston, Bristol, Cambridge, Kent, and Lancaster were named after towns and counties in England.

The English also named cities in honor of their kings, queens, and nobility. Jamestown, Virginia, an early colony, is named after King James I. New York is named in honor of the Duke of York, brother of King Charles II.

The names of English explorers are also found on the map of the United States. Henry Hudson sailed up the East Coast and into the river later named in his honor. Pennsylvania honors its founder, the Quaker leader William Penn. Baltimore, Maryland, is named after its founder, Lord Baltimore.

French Place-Names

French explorers and settlers also named places after French cities, kings, and explorers. New Orleans is named after the French city of **Orléans,** saved by the heroic Joan of Arc, who led the French army against an English invasion. Louisiana was named for King Louis XIV, the king of France when the territory of Louisiana was explored and claimed by French explorers.

Provo, Utah, was named after Étienne Provost, a French-Canadian fur trader. Des Moines, Iowa, means "of the monks" in French and refers to the Catholic missionaries who explored the area. Lake Champlain, in New York, is named for its discoverer, Samuel Champlain.

The French gave many descriptive names to places they discovered or founded. Boise, Idaho, comes from the French word for "woods." Presque Isle, in Pennsylvania, Maine, and Michigan, means "almost an island." Eau Claire, Wisconsin, means "clear water"; Fond du Lac, in Wisconsin and Minnesota, means "far end of the lake"; and Belle Plaine, Iowa, means "beautiful plain."

The word **ville** in French means "city" or "town." As with the word **town** in Jamestown and Englishtown, the word **ville** was added to other words to come up with names of towns: Knoxville and Nashville in Tennessee; Belleville, La Fargeville, and Depauville in northern New York.

Italian, Greek, Latin, and German Influences

Spanish, English, French, and Indian words are the main sources of names of places in the United States, but there are others. America was named after the Italian explorer Amerigo Vespucci, who determined that the Americas were a separate continent from Asia.

Many American places were named after places and people of ancient Greek and Roman civilizations: Seneca, Ithaca, Carthage, Euclid. Philadelphia means "city of brotherly love" in Greek. Agricola, a town name in several states, means "farmer" in Latin. German settlers gave their new Missouri home a Latin name, Concordia, meaning "concord" or "peace."

Many cities in Pennsylvania end with the word **burg** or **burgh,** German for "castle" or "fort": Pittsburgh, Harrisburg, Strasburg, Mechanicsburg. Gothenburg, in Nebraska, the site of an old Pony Express station, was named for a city in Sweden.

Further Study

We could go on and on with the study of the origins of American place-names. The richness and diversity of the population in the United States are evident in the great variety of place-names. Remember, early settlers had an enormous new country to name. They used the languages and the names of places they knew. Settlers far away from home probably felt less homesick when surrounded by familiar place-names.

When you see the name of a city or a street, a river or a lake, a state or a county, ask yourself what language it may have come from. You may find the origin and story of place-names in dictionaries of American place-names in your local or school library. Why don't you start by finding the story of the name of your street, city, county, or state?

Activity F

1. List three Spanish place-names with their English meanings.

_____

2. Who lived in what is now the United States before any Europeans came?

_____

3. List three states with Indian names.

_____

4. Name three American cities that have been named for places in England.

_____

5. For whom is New York named?

_____

6. What do the French word **ville** and the German word **burg** mean? Can you find two cities in your area that end with **ville** and two that end with **burg?**

_____

7. List three French place-names with their English meanings.

_____

8. After whom is America named?

_____

Resources and References

History of Language

Beowulf. Trans. Howell D. Chickering, Jr. Garden City, NY: Anchor Press/Doubleday, 1977.

Beowulf. Trans. Charles W. Kennedy. Eleventh Printing. New York: Oxford University Press, 1962.

Cahn, William, and Cahn, Rhoda. *The Story of Writing*. Harvey House, 1963.

Charlin, Remy; Beth, Mary; and Ancona, George. *Handtalk: An ABC of Finger Spelling and Sign Language*. Parents' Magazine Press, 1974.

Chaucer, Geoffrey. *The Riverside Chaucer*. Larry D. Benson, ed. Boston: Houghton Mifflin, 1987.

Davidson, Jessica. *Is That Mother in the Bottle? Where Language Came From and Where It Is Going*. New York: Watts, 1972.

Davidson, Marshall, ed. *Great Civilizations of the Past: Golden Book of Lost Worlds*. New York: Golden Books, 1962.

Epstein, Sam, and Epstein, Beryl. *All About Prehistoric Cave Men*. New York: Random House, 1959.

Ernst, Margaret. *Words: English Roots and How They Grew*. NY: Harper and Row, 1982.

Gannette, Henry. *The Origin of Certain Place Names in the United States*. Detroit: Gale Research Company, 1971.

Harder, Kelsie B. *Illustrated Dictionary of Place Names*. New York: Van Nostrand Reinhold, 1976.

Longman, Harold. *What's Behind the Word?* New York: Perl, Coward-McCann, 1968.

Pei, Mario. *The Story of Language*. Philadelphia: J.B. Lippincott, 1984.

Rogers, Frances. *Painted Rock to Printed Page: History of Printing and Communication*. Philadelphia: Lippincott, 1960.

Scott, Joseph, and Scott, Lenore. *Egyptian Hieroglyphs for Everyone: An Introduction to the Writing of Ancient Egypt*. New York: Funk and Wagnalls, 1968.

The World Book Encyclopedia. Chicago: World Book, Inc., 1994.

Foreign Countries

Balerdi, Susan. *France: The Crossroads of Europe*. Dillon Press, 1984. For younger readers.

Bradley, Catherine. *Germany: The Reunification of a Nation*. Gloucester Press, 1991. For younger readers.

Farfield, Sheila. *Peoples and Nations of Africa*. Gareth Stevens, 1988.

Georges, D.V. *South America*. Children's Press, 1986.

James, Ian. *Italy*. Watts, 1988. For younger readers.

Miller, Arthur. *Spain*. Chelsea House, 1988. For younger readers.

Resources and References *(continued)*

Filmstrips

Ancient Civilizations. National Geographic Society.
Christmas in France. Huntsville, TX: Educational Filmstrips.
Christmas in Germany. Huntsville, TX: Educational Filmstrips.
Christmas in Spain. Huntsville, TX: Educational Filmstrips.
France. Huntsville, TX: Educational Filmstrips.
Germany, West and East. Niles, IL: United Learning.
Glimpses of West Africa. Gessler Publishing Co.
Let's Visit Mexico. Pleasantville, NY: EAV.
Let's Visit South America. Pleasantville, NY: EAV.
Let's Visit Spain. Pleasantville, NY: EAV.
Martinique et Guadeloupe. Gessler Publishing Co.

Pedagogy

Curtain, A., and Pesola, Ann C. *Languages and Children—Making the Match.* Addison-Wesley, 1988.

Kennedy, D., and De Lorenzo, W.E. *Complete Guide to Exploratory Foreign Language Programs.* Lincolnwood, IL: National Textbook Company, 1985.

Raven, P.T. *FLEX: A Foreign Language Experience.* ERIC Document No. ED 238 301, 1983.

Seelye, H. Ned. *Teaching Culture.* Lincolnwood, IL: National Textbook Co., 1984.

Dictionaries

(All Amsco School Publications, New York)

The New College French & English Dictionary, 1988.
The New College German & English Dictionary, 1981.
The New College Italian & English Dictionary, 1976.
The New College Latin & English Dictionary, 1994.
The New College Spanish & English Dictionary, 1987.

To the Student

You are about to embark on a journey of discovery — beginning to learn a new language spoken by millions of people around the world, SPANISH.

Learning Spanish provides an opportunity to explore another language and culture. Spanish may be one of several languages you will discover in this course. You can then select which language you will continue to study.

Whatever your goals, this book will be a fun beginning in exploring a special gift you have as a human being: the ability to speak a language other than your own. The more you learn how to communicate with other people, the better you will be able to live and work in the world around you.

In this book, you will discover the Spanish language and the world where it is spoken. The Spanish words and expressions you will learn have been limited so that you will feel at ease.

You will learn how to express many things in Spanish: how to greet people, how to count, how to tell the day and month of the year, how to identify and describe many objects, and more.

You will use Spanish to talk about yourself and your friends. You will practice with many different activities, like puzzles and word games, Spanish songs, cartoons, and pictures. Some activities you will do with classmates or with the whole class. You will act out skits and conversations and sing Spanish songs. You will learn about many interesting bits of Spanish culture: school days, holidays, leisure time, sports, and interesting manners and customs.

You will also meet young Conchita, who will be your guide on how to pronounce Spanish words. Look for Conchita's clues throughout this book and get a feel for the Spanish language, its sounds, and its musical quality. You will also develop an ear for Spanish, so listen carefully to your teacher and the cassettes.

You will quickly realize that learning a new language is not as hard as you might have imagined. Enjoy using it with your teacher and classmates. Try not to be shy or afraid of making mistakes when speaking: remember, the more you speak, the more you will learn. And you can even show off the Spanish you learn to family, relatives, and friends. After all, learning a new language means talking with the rest of the world and with each other.

Now — on to Spanish. **¡Buena suerte!**, which means *Good luck!*

— *K.R.A.*

Contents

Spain, Spanish America, and the Spanish Language

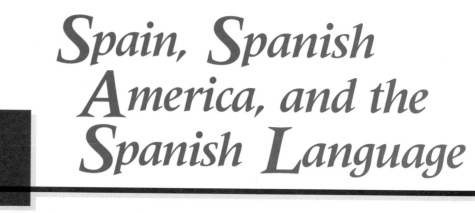

1

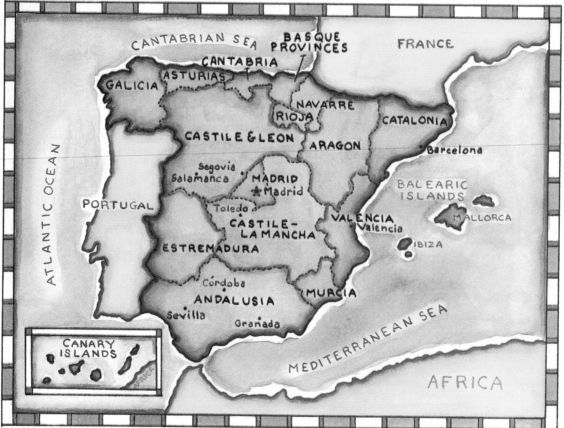

Spanish is one of the major Romance languages that evolved from the Indo-European family of languages. It is the language of 300 million people in 21 countries and the fourth most widely spoken language in the world. Although these Spanish-speaking countries share a common language, they are different from one another: each has its own form of government, economic system, monetary currency, customs, and traditions particular to its people and history.

NOTE TO TEACHERS

➡ Be sure not to rush through the introduction or the cultural sections, **Rincón cultural.** Students are always intrigued by foreign lands and cultures. They ask many questions about cultural differences and remember cultural details long after they may have forgotten language and grammatical points.

➡ Take time to study the art and maps in the book and supplement the text with postcards and magazines, travel brochures, posters, souvenirs and artifacts, slides, photographs, and video materials. You may have students find some of these materials themselves. Relatives, friends, libraries, travel agencies, consulates of Spanish-speaking countries, and cultural entities are excellent sources for students to contact. Set up a classroom bulletin board or have students create a collage in the shape of Central and South America and Spain on which to display postcards, photos, and so on.

➡ Students also love to hear personal stories and anecdotes. If possible, provide authentic and personalized information about Hispanic culture by relating your own stories or inviting a native or someone who has visited a Spanish-speaking country to speak to students and answer questions.

➡ Bring photographs to class to illustrate racial and ethnic diversity among the people of Spanish-speaking countries. You may wish to solicit authentic photographs from students who have Hispanic relatives or friends.

Rincón cultural (Supplementary Culture)

➡ Most countries of Spanish America have populations of several different racial groups:

◆ **Whites:** Descendants of the Spanish settlers and of later European immigrants (from Italy, Germany, England, Ireland, and the Slavic countries). In Argentina and Uruguay the population is mostly white.

◆ **Indians:** Found in great numbers in most Spanish-American countries, especially in Mexico, Ecuador, Bolivia, and Peru. Most are descendants of two ancient Indian civilizations, the Aztecs (Mexico) and the Incas (Peru, Ecuador, and Bolivia).

◆ **Mestizos** (people of mixed Spanish and Indian blood): In many Spanish-American countries these are the largest single group.

◆ **Blacks:** The descendants of Africans who were brought to Spanish America for heavy labor in colonial days. They are most numerous in the West Indies, in the Caribbean.

◆ **Mulattos** (people of mixed Spanish and African blood): They are most numerous in the West Indies, Venezuela, and Colombia.

Rincón cultural (Supplementary Culture)

➡ Students may be interested to learn more about Christopher Columbus, one of the most recognized names in history.

◆ Christopher Columbus was born in Genoa, Italy, of Spanish parents. By the age of fourteen, he had decided to dedicate his life to the sea. An outstanding navigator and explorer, Columbus was fascinated by the idea of reaching Asia—famous for spices, jewelry, silk, and gold. In the latter 1400s, the Ottoman Turks controlled most of southeast Europe, cutting off easy access to Asia via an easterly route. Although at that time many European countries were attempting to reach Asia by sailing around Africa, Columbus had a different plan. Columbus's calculations convinced him that the easiest route to Asia lay 3,900 miles west of Spain, across the Atlantic Ocean, in the direction of what is today Central America.

◆ To carry out his project, Columbus needed a sponsor to provide the money, ships, and sailors for such a long and risky journey. His personality, as well as the danger of the route, made it extremely difficult to find a sponsor. In 1486, after being rejected by the king of Portugal, Columbus solicited support from King Ferdinand and Queen Isabella of Spain. The king and queen initially refused to sponsor the voyage. Finally, Columbus convinced the intensely religious monarchs that the voyage would not only enrich Spain with a wealth of goods and gold but also aid in spreading Christianity around the world. On August 3, 1492, Columbus set sail on three ships, the *Niña,* the *Pinta,* and the *Santa María.* On October 12, after a long and hard journey, the ships landed on an island in the Caribbean Sea. Columbus and his crew were convinced they had landed near Japan or China.

Spanish is the official language of Spain, including the Canary and the Baleares Islands.

Spain, slightly smaller than the state of Texas, has 40 million inhabitants. Situated at the western edge of the European continent, Spain borders on France to the north-east and Portugal to the west. Three of its sides border on water: the Mediterranean Sea, the Cantabrian Sea, and the Atlantic Ocean.

Most Spanish words derive from Latin, but many words are of Arabic origin as a consequence of the Moorish occupation of Spain from the eighth to the fifteenth centuries. This period, lasting seven centuries and sometimes called the Reconquest, was marked by conflict and wars between the Moors and the Christians of the Spanish Kingdoms. The Reconquest proved to be such a long struggle because the various Spanish Kingdoms were not united and each fought for its own interests and territory. Finally, in 1492, King Ferdinand and Queen Isabella completed the reconquest of the Spanish Kingdoms, expelled the Moors, and for the first time united Christian Spain as a country. 1492 was also the year the King and Queen sponsored Christopher Columbus's expedition to the Americas.

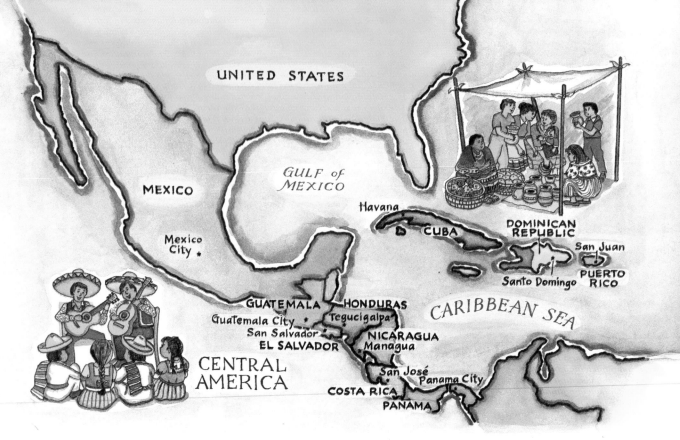

By the end of the fifteenth century, Spain had become a major world power. With its mighty fleet, Spain began her great exploration and colonization of Central and South America. Spanish became the dominant language of the territories settled by the Spaniards. Today, Spanish is the official language of more than 240 million people living in what may be called Spanish America. Spanish America includes Mexico and eighteen countries located in Central America, South America, and the Caribbean.

There are also 20 million Spanish-speaking people in the United States, giving the U.S. the fourth largest Spanish-speaking population in the world. In some American cities in Texas, New Mexico, Arizona, California, New York, and Florida, the concentration of Spanish speakers is so high that Hispanics represent more than half the population. Most Americans of Hispanic origin came from Mexico, Cuba, and Puerto Rico, although there are also large numbers of immigrants from the Dominican Republic, Colombia, and Nicaragua.

Rincón cultural (Supplementary Culture)

➡ The lands discovered by Columbus in the name of Spain became Spanish territories. Having accumulated vast territories in the Americas, the king and queen now needed brave and determined men to explore and settle the new lands.

➡ Here are some of the most famous Spanish explorers:

- ◆ **Hernán Cortés** and **Francisco Pizarro** are two of the best-known explorers because they conquered the two most advanced Indian civilizations in the Americas. Cortés conquered the last Aztec emperor, Moctezuma, and Pizarro defeated the last Inca emperor, Atahualpa.

- ◆ **Juan Ponce de León** established the first Spanish colony in Puerto Rico and discovered what is now Florida in his search for the "Fountain of Youth."

- ◆ **Vasco Núñez de Balboa** crossed the Isthmus of Panama and in 1513 discovered the Pacific Ocean, which he called **Mar del Sur** *(South Sea).*

- ◆ **Francisco Vásquez de Coronado** explored Mexico and what is now the Southwest of the United States. He also discovered the Grand Canyon.

- ◆ **Alvar Núñez Cabeza de Vaca** explored Florida, the Mississippi, and northern Mexico.

➡ With the explorers, many missionaries also came to the New World to spread Christianity.

Note to Teachers

➡ Have students learn more about Spain and Spanish-speaking countries by doing research projects, either as written or oral reports.

- ◆ Topics for research may involve choosing a Spanish-speaking country and finding its size, population, capital city, bordering countries, language(s) spoken besides Spanish, colors of the flag (see Note to Teachers, page 46), currency used, typical foods and dishes, holidays, dress, music, and so on. Prepare guiding questions to help focus students' attention on the topic chosen.

- ◆ Have students bring maps, photographs from travel brochures or magazines, authentic photographs taken by friends or relatives, souvenirs, and music.

- ◆ Whenever possible, have students bring books or magazines to illustrate what the people of the country look and dress like.

CARIBBEAN SEA

Caracas
VENEZUELA

★Bogotá
COLOMBIA

Quito★
ECUADOR

PERU

SOUTH AMERICA

★Lima

BOLIVIA
★La Paz

PARAGUAY

CHILE

★Asunción

ARGENTINA

URUGUAY

Santiago ★

Buenos Aires★

★Montevideo

PACIFIC OCEAN

ATLANTIC OCEAN

Many civilizations flourished in Spanish America before the arrival of the Spaniards in the fifteenth century, primarily the Mayas, Aztecs, and Incas. Ruins in Mexico, Guatemala, and Peru attest to the greatness and ingenuity of these peoples, who left a rich testament of their artistic accomplishments in architecture, sculpture, murals, and jewelry.

In the fifteenth century, the region of Castilla was the most powerful of the Spanish Kingdoms: its language, Castilian, became the official language of the country. Although Castilian Spanish is still the official language of Spain, Spaniards of certain regions of Spain also speak different regional languages or dialects, such as **catalán**, **gallego**, and **vascuense**, an ancient language unrelated to any other on earth.

The Spaniards who settled in Spanish America came mostly from a region in southern Spain called **Andalucía**. They brought to the lands they settled what may be called *Andalusian* Spanish. The main difference between Castilian and Andalusian Spanish is the pronunciation of **c** (before **e** or **i**) and the **z** sound. In Castilian, the **c** of **cero** and the **z** of **zebra** are both pronounced like *th*. In Andalusian, the letters **c** and **z** are both pronounced with the *s* sound.

There are 28 letters in the Spanish alphabet. The letters **k** and **w** do not exist in Spanish, although they may be found in words borrowed from other languages. The Spanish alphabet contains the additional letters **ch**, **ñ**, **ll**, and **rr**.

Rincón cultural (Supplementary Culture)

You may wish to provide more information on the Inca, Aztec, and Maya civilizations to students.

➡ Although it is commonly said that Columbus discovered the New World, one must not forget that before his arrival, great civilizations had existed in the Americas for centuries. Many of these cultures have left evidence of their knowledge and achievement in the fields of astronomy, physics, mathematics, and engineering. How they attained such a high degree of development is still unknown.

➡ The following were among the most advanced Amerindian (American Indian) civilizations in Central and South America:

◆ The **Incas** created the greatest empire in the New World. They controlled roughly 5,000 miles stretching from Ecuador to central Chile. By the time the Spaniards arrived, the empire's population numbered approximately 6 million. The Incas were excellent architects and engineers. They built huge buildings, bridges, aqueducts, and stone-paved highways connecting the different parts of the empire. The Incas used massive blocks of stone, weighing as much as 300 tons each, for their constructions. How the Incas transported these huge stones without the wheel or the aid of powerful animals is still a mystery. The stones were also cut and shaped without the use of iron tools. The blocks fit so tightly together without cement that to this day a knife blade cannot be inserted between them.

◆ The **Aztecs,** originally hunters and farmers, settled in the Valley of Mexico and created an empire that included central and southern Mexico and extended from the Atlantic to the Pacific coast. They were excellent goldsmiths, jewelers, and artisans. The Aztecs are also famous for their extraordinary military skills, which helped them expand their empire.

◆ The **Mayas** were the most brilliant and advanced of the pre-Columbian civilizations. Their empire extended from the Yucatán Peninsula, in Mexico, to Central America. By the time the Spaniards arrived in America, the Mayas had long disappeared, but they left many traces of their superior civilization. The Mayas developed advanced mathematics and an efficient writing system. They also developed an extremely accurate calendar which rivals calendars in use today. The Mayas were also great astronomers. With the aid of observatories, temples, and pyramids, they marked the movements of the sun, the moon, and many stars. Maya astronomers were even capable of predicting solar eclipses.

The exact causes of the fall of the Maya empire are still not known. Some attribute their disappearance to social unrest or revolutions, others to a major natural catastrophe.

Rincón cultural (Supplementary Culture)

➡ You may wish to familiarize students with the variety of dishes of the Spanish-speaking world.

From Spain:

- **caldo gallego:** thick vegetable, sausage, and ham soup
- **churros:** long deep-fried doughnuts covered with sugar
- **empanadas:** spicy meat, fish, or chicken pies
- **flan:** egg custard dessert
- **gazpacho:** chilled tomato soup
- **paella:** yellow rice prepared with seafood, chicken, sausages, and spices
- **tortilla española:** potato and onion omelet

From Spanish America:

- **ajiaco bogotano:** creamed chicken and potato soup with avocado and capers
- **arroz blanco con frijoles** or **habichuelas:** white rice and beans
- **arroz con pollo:** yellow rice with chicken
- **ceviche:** fresh raw fish, marinated in lime/lemon juice with red onions and hot chilies
- **hallacas:** corn dough with meat and vegetable filling, steamed in banana leaves
- **lechón asado:** roasted pork
- **mole poblano:** a sauce made of chocolate, nuts, and chilies served with turkey, chicken, or pork
- **sancocho:** thick soup made with beef, plantains, yucca, and other tropical roots
- **tostones:** slices of green plantains, deep-fried, flattened, and refried until crispy

In the same way that American English words and expressions have changed from British English (**lift** = *elevator*, **flat** = *apartment*), so the Spanish spoken in different parts of the world has differing vocabulary. For example, a Puerto Rican ordering a **china** (*orange*) in Spain would not be understood by a Spaniard, who calls an orange a **naranja**. A **papa** (*potato*) in Mexico is called a **patata** in Spain.

Food also varies from country to country in the Spanish-speaking world. You are probably most familiar with dishes from Mexico. **Tacos**, **tamales**, **enchiladas**, and **burritos** all originated in Mexico. They are all rich in beans and corn, crops grown by those who inhabited Mexico before Columbus. From Hispanic countries in the Caribbean come **tostones** (*fried green plantains*) and **empanadillas** (*meat-filled turnovers*). Pork and seafood, beans, corn, and patatoes are important ingredients of Hispanic cooking (in the Andes there are more than thirty varieties of potatoes). A favorite Spanish dish is **paella**, a combination of rice, seafood, chicken, and sausages served with vegetables and spices.

The great tradition of Spanish literature continues to influence contemporary writers. Perhaps you have seen pictures of a tall, skinny knight battling windmills. He is Don Quijote, a creation of the writer Miguel de Cervantes, who lived in sixteenth-century Spain. Don Quijote rode Rocinante, a broken-down horse, and traveled with his short, fat friend, Sancho Panza, as they searched for adventure.

In the twentieth century, many Hispanic novelists have reached international acclaim, among them Octavio Paz, Gabriel García Márquez, Pablo Neruda, and Carlos Fuentes. Also of the twentieth century, three outstanding Spanish painters are Pablo Picasso, Salvador Dalí, and Joan Miró. Many of their paintings hang in the Prado, a beautiful art museum in Madrid, Spain.

Spanish-speaking countries also have many popular art forms. Music, for example, is a rich component of everyday life in Spain and Spanish America. Much of the popular music is based on traditional and folkloristic themes. Perhaps you have heard some of the exciting rhythms from the Spanish-speaking world: mariachi music from Mexico, the rumba, merengue, and mambo from the Caribbean, the tango from Argentina, and flamenco from Spain and Spanish America.

Fiestas or popular festivals are also a Spanish tradition very much alive in Spain and Hispanic countries. Each region, no matter how small, has its own festival, celebrated in honor of a saint for whom the town feels a particular devotion. These festivals include parades, lively music, and dancing in the streets, where tempting food specialties of the region may be sampled at every corner. Another type of festival, also considered a sport, is the bullfight. It is popular not only in Spain but also in other Hispanic countries. The tradition of bullfighting can be traced back to very ancient times.

Now — on to the study of this beautiful and influential language. Have fun and enjoy it!

Rincón cultural (Supplementary Culture)

Music of Spain and Spanish America

➡ Among the many musical styles that form the Spanish musical tradition, **flamenco** is probably the best-known. This style, developed by the Gypsies, is a blend of Arabic, Jewish, and Gypsy rhythms expressed in song and dance. The special **flamenco** singing, known as **cante hondo** (*deep chant*), shows influence from Muslim religious chants. In **flamenco** dancing, men in tight black suits and heeled boots perform amazing steps that involve complicated toe-and-heel taps on the ground, while women in colorful dresses with frilled skirts dance with expressive hand and body movements. Hand claps and castanets add rhythm to the guitar accompaniment.

➡ Of all Spanish musical instruments, the **guitarra** (*guitar*) is the most important. The guitar, which dates back to the sixteenth century, is a Spanish invention based on a medieval string instrument used by the Moors. The **castañuelas** (*castanets*), brought to Spain by the Phoenicians, are also commonly used in Spanish music.

➡ When brought to the New World, the rich Spanish musical styles blended with the music of the Amerindian cultures and later, with African music. Among the various Spanish-American musical styles, some of the most famous are the **salsa** from the Caribbean, the **corrido** from Mexico, the **joropo** from Venezuela, and the **tango** from Argentina. During the latter part of the twentieth century, a new musical style was created: **jazz afrocubano**, or *Latin jazz*, a blend of American jazz and Afro-Cuban or Caribbean rhythms.

➡ Music from Spanish America includes the guitar as well as many Amerindian instruments:

- ◆ **güiro:** a hollow pumpkinlike fruit
- ◆ **quena:** a wooden flute used by the Incas
- ◆ **maracas:** a hollow pumpkinlike fruit containing pebbles or seeds
- ◆ **clave:** two short sticks struck together

➡ African percussion instruments also contributed to Hispanic music:

- ◆ **conga:** a large cylindrical drum
- ◆ **bongo:** a pair of small drums played together
- ◆ **batá:** a drum shaped like an hourglass

➡ Spanish-American traditional dances are as numerous and varied as the music. Some common dances are the **tango** from Argentina, the **bomba** and the **plena** from Puerto Rico, the **merengue** from the Dominican Republic, and the **cumbia** from Colombia. **Salsa** is a contemporary dance born from Afro-Cuban and Caribbean rhythms like the **rumba**, the **mambo**, and the **guaracha**.

ANSWERS TO ACTIVIDAD

1. *King Ferdinand and Queen Isabella of Spain*

2. *Spanish became the dominant language because the Spaniards colonized and settled in Central and South America.*

3. *in Central America: El Salvador, Panama, Guatemala, Honduras, Nicaragua, Costa Rica; in the Caribbean: Cuba, Dominican Republic, and Puerto Rico*

4. *South America*

5. *the United States*

6. *of the Mayas, of the Aztecs, and of the Incas*

7. *catalán, gallego, and vascuense*

8. *Both are pronounced like th.*

9. *twenty-eight letters*

10. *Paella is a combination of rice, seafood, chicken, and sausages cooked with vegetables and spices.*

11. *A character created by the Spanish writer Miguel de Cervantes. He lived in the sixteenth century and traveled with his friend, Sancho Panza, in search of adventure.*

12. *Pablo Picasso, Salvador Dalí, and Joan Miró*

1. Who sponsored Christopher Columbus's expedition to the Americas?

_____

2. Why is Spanish spoken in Central and South America? _____

_____

3. Look at the map on page 4 and name the Spanish-speaking countries of

Central America and the Caribbean. _____

_____

4. Which continent has the greatest number of Spanish-speaking countries?

_____

5. Which country has the fourth largest Spanish-speaking population?

_____

6. Name three civilizations that flourished in Spanish America before the

fifteenth century. _____

7. Name three regional languages or dialects spoken in Spain.

_____

8. How do you pronounce the letters **c** and **z** in Castilian Spanish?

_____

9. How many letters does the Spanish alphabet contain? _____

10. What is **paella**? _____

11. Who is Don Quijote? _____

12. Name three twentieth-century Spanish painters. _____

_____

2 Spanish Cognates

You already know many Spanish words. Some of the words are spelled exactly like English words. In many other words, the only difference between Spanish and English is one or two letters. Here are some clues to watch for. Spanish **f** is equivalent to English *ph*: **foto** = *photo*, **teléfono** = *telephone*; words ending in **-ción** in Spanish often end in *-tion* in English: **generación** = *generation*, **internacional** = *international*; words ending in **-dad** in Spanish frequently end in *-ty* in English: **realidad** = *reality*, **actividad** = *activity*. You will also find words like **automóvil,** where Spanish **v** is replaced by English *b*. In Spanish, the letters **b** and **v** are both pronounced like a soft *b*.

How many of the following Spanish words can you recognize? Fill in the blanks with the English meanings. If you need to, you may look in a dictionary. Listen to your teacher or the cassette for the pronunciation of these words:

1. actriz _____

2. aire _____

3. arte _____

4. artista _____

5. automóvil _____

6. banco _____

7. béisbol _____

8. bicicleta _____

9. calculadora _____

10. canoa _____

11. chocolate _____

12. científico _____

13. clase _____

14. concierto _____

15. crema _____

16. delicioso _____

17. dentista _____

18. diferente _____

Cognates provide a perfect opportunity to delight students with early discovery of words they can easily associate with what they already know.

ANSWERS TO ACTIVIDAD

1. *actress*
2. *air*
3. *art*
4. *artist*
5. *automobile*
6. *bank*
7. *baseball*
8. *bicycle*
9. *calculator*
10. *canoe*
11. *chocolate*
12. *scientific*
13. *class*
14. *concert*
15. *cream*
16. *delicious*
17. *dentist*
18. *different*

ANSWERS TO ACTIVIDAD (continued)

19. *Europe*
20. *excellent*
21. *fabulous*
22. *family*
23. *fantastic*
24. *favorite*
25. *photo*
26. *fruit*
27. *generation*
28. *geography*
29. *globe*
30. *gorilla*
31. *group*
32. *guitar*
33. *hamburger*
34. *hurricane*
35. *important*
36. *independent*
37. *international*
38. *laboratory*
39. *map*
40. *mathematics*
41. *north*

42. *office*
43. *pilot*
44. *possible*
45. *telephone*
46. *tiger*
47. *tomato*
48. *train*
49. *trumpet*
50. *volleyball*

NOTE TO TEACHERS

You may want students to look at the advertisements on page 11 and guess the meanings of the Spanish words that have English cognates.

19. Europa _____

20. excelente _____

21. fabuloso _____

22. familia _____

23. fantástico _____

24. favorito _____

25. foto _____

26. fruta _____

27. generación _____

28. geografía _____

29. globo _____

30. gorila _____

31. grupo _____

32. guitarra _____

33. hamburguesa _____

34. huracán _____

35. importante _____

36. independiente _____

37. internacional _____

38. laboratorio _____

39. mapa _____

40. matemáticas _____

41. norte _____

42. oficina _____

43. piloto _____

44. posible _____

45. teléfono _____

46. tigre _____

47. tomate _____

48. tren _____

49. trompeta _____

50. volibol _____

El Cine Popular
presenta
EL TIGRE EN BICICLETA
con el fabuloso actor
☆ Antonio Casas ☆

¡Viernes Internacional!
CONCIERTO de GUITARRA
Música original de España el 6 de mayo
Conservatorio Municipal

¡MI FAMILIA FAVORITA!
¡La comedia de una nueva generación! en el Teatro Moderno

3 | Spanish Names

Now that you are able to recognize over 50 Spanish words resembling English, let's look at how Spanish and English names compare.

Conchita is going to help you learn how to pronounce some of these names.

You will meet **Conchita** throughout this book holding her lens over one or two pronunciation clues she wants to share with you as you develop a good Spanish pronunciation.

Whenever you look at **Conchita**'s clues, keep this in mind: every time you try to pronounce a Spanish sound, hold your mouth, tongue, lips, and teeth in the same position at the end of the sound as you did at the beginning. Try saying **o** this way. Now try **oooo**. There, you've got it.

Conchita has two clues for you before you listen to the following list of boys' and girls' names. These clues will tell you how to pronounce HER name:

Alfonso, Carlos

➡ In each section, students encounter **Conchita,** a young Spanish detective, who will teach them pronunciation skills. Emphasize the phonetic concepts **Conchita** presents. Model all Spanish words for students and/or have them listen to the cassette. Have students repeat individually and in unison.

➡ To teach and practice the Spanish sounds **Conchita** presents in the book, you may wish to illustrate on cards two or three words containing the sounds introduced. Use the cards throughout the course to review sounds already studied.

➡ To have more fun with **Conchita** and her clues, bring an oversized jacket and hat to class. Have students play **Conchita,** wearing the jacket and hat as they model the sounds and words of **Conchita's** clues to the class.

➡ Children love to be able to say the alphabet. You may reproduce the alphabet below for students and have the class repeat the alphabet several times, gaining speed with each repetition.

Alphabet

Letter	Name	Sound	Example
a	a	*a* in *father*	**papel** (*paper*)
b	be	*b* in *boy*	**boca** (*mouth*)
c	ce	*c* in *civil* before *e, i*	**cinco** (*five*)
		c in *cat* before *a, o, u*	**cuatro** (*four*)
ch	che	*ch* in *church*	**muchacho** (*boy*)
d	de	*d* in *dog*	**día** (*day*)
e	e	*e* in *they*	**enero** (*January*)
f	efe	*f* in *fine*	**febrero** (*February*)
g	ge	*h* in *hay* before *e, i*	**genio** (*genius*)
		g in *game* before *a, o, u*	**domingo** (*Sunday*)
h	hache	silent	**¡Hola!** (*Hi!*)
i	i	*i* in *police*	**abril** (*April*)
j	jota	*h* in *home*	**julio** (*July*)
k	ka	*k* in *kid*	**kilómetro** (*kilometer*)
l	ele	*l* in *little*	**lápiz** (*pencil*)
ll	elle	*y* in *yellow* or *j* in *jet*	**silla** (*chair*)
m	eme	*m* in *miss*	**mano** (*hand*)
n	ene	*n* in *now*	**nariz** (*nose*)
ñ	eñe	*n* in *onion*	**español** (Spanish)
o	o	*o* in *old*	**ojo** (*eye*)

Alphabet (continued)

Letter	Name	Sound	Example
p	pe	*p* in *puppy*	**puerta** (*door*)
q	cu	*k* in *kid*	**quien** (*who*)
r	ere	single trill	**rojo** (*red*)
rr	erre	longer trill	**pizarra** (*chalkboard*)
s	ese	*s* in *sea*	**sí** (*yes*)
t	te	*t* in *sting*	**tiza** (*chalk*)
u	u	*u* in *tune*	**uno** (*one*)
v	uve	*b* in *boy*	**verde** (*green*)
w	doble ve	found only in foreign words	
x	equis	*ks* in *sacks* before vowels	**exacto** (*exact*)
y	ye	*y* in *you* or *j* in *jet*	**yo** (*I*)
z	zeta	*s* in *soup*	**brazo** (*arm*)

NOTE TO TEACHERS

➡ Have each student choose a Spanish name. For additional names, students may consult the name day calendar on page 17. Here are the Spanish names on the list that do not resemble English, along with some English equivalents:

BOYS

Carlos	*Charles*	**Guillermo**	*William*	**Lorenzo**	*Lawrence*
Claudio	*no equivalent*	**Jaime**	*James*	**Miguel**	*Michael*
Diego	*Douglas*	**José**	*Joseph*	**Pablo**	*Paul*
Enrique	*Henry*	**Juan**	*John*	**Pedro**	*Peter*
Esteban	*Steven*	**Julio**	*Jules*	**Ramón**	*Raymond*

GIRLS

Catalina	*Katherine*	**Inés**	*no equivalent*	**Juana**	*Joan*

➡ Have students make name tags for the Spanish names they have chosen. Students may write **Me llamo** before their Spanish names.

Here is a list of boys' and girls' names. With your teacher's help, choose a Spanish name that you would like to have for yourself while you are studying Spanish:

Alberto	Felipe	Gabriel	Jaime	Julio
Alejandro	Fernando	Gilberto	José (Pepe)	Lorenzo
Alfonso	Francisco (Paco)	Guillermo	Juan	Luis
Andrés				Manuel
Antonio				Marcos
Benjamín				Miguel
Carlos				Nicolás
Claudio				Pablo
David				Pedro
Diego				Rafael
Eduardo				Ramón
Enrique				Ricardo
Ernesto				Roberto
Esteban				Tomás
Federico				Víctor

Adela	Emilia	Gloria	Isabel	Laura
Alberta	Estela	Inés	Josefina	Leonor
Alicia	Eva	Irene	Juana	Lucía
Ana María				Luisa
Ana				Magdalena
Bárbara				Margarita
Beatriz				María
Carlota				(Mariucha)
Carmen				Patricia
Carolina				Rosalía
Catalina				Sara
Cecilia				Sofía
Dolores				Susana
Elena				Teresa
Elisa				Virginia

When Spanish speakers want to say, "My name is Pilar," they say, **"Me llamo Pilar."** Practice telling your teacher and your classmates your name in Spanish. If you and your teacher have chosen Spanish names, use them.

Conchita's clues:

e = e in met

i = ee in deed

u = u in put

Elisa, bu**e**no

ad**ió**s, d**í**as

mucho **gu**sto

➡ This **Actividad** gives students immediate experience in using the language. If students have made Spanish name tags, use them.

- ◆ Point to yourself and say, **"Me llamo _____ (your name)."**

- ◆ Then point to a student and ask, **"¿Cómo te llamas?"** If the student does not understand, repeat your name. Model **"Me llamo"** again until the student catches on.

➡ At this point, you may wish to introduce expressions students will later see in written form in the dialogs:

- ◆ Point to a student and say, **"Se llama _____."**

- ◆ Ask another student, **"¿Cómo se llama?"**

Repeat these four phrases with several students, giving as many as possible a chance to participate.

You can find the English meanings of all Spanish phrases in the end Vocabulary. All Spanish materials are included in the cassette program.

➡ *Conchita's clues:* Model pronunciation of the Spanish **e, i,** and **u** sounds for students. You may wish to refer students to the list of names on page 13 to find and pronounce additional words containing these sounds.

NOTE TO TEACHERS

➡ Before students are asked to read **Diálogo** 1 for meaning, have them look at the characters and guess what Elisa and Jaime may be saying to each other in each illustration.

➡ Next, model pronunciation either by reading aloud or by playing the cassette while students read the dialog.

➡ Have students close their books. Read short segments for students to repeat. If a phrase is too long, break it into shorter sections, reading the last part first. Have students repeat, then add another word or two until you have read the entire segment. Have students repeat after each addition. For example:

¿Y tú?
Jaime. ¿Y tú?
Me llamo Jaime. ¿Y tú?

➡ Ask questions:

◆ How does the boy say hello?

◆ What does the girl ask the boy?

◆ What is the boy's name?

◆ Are they happy to meet each other?

◆ What do they say to each other?

◆ How do they say good-bye?

➡ Note that the optional dialog, **Diálogo** 4, **"Buenas noches,"** introducing **usted,** is included on page 55 of the Teacher Annotations. You may reproduce it for your students if you wish to teach the **usted** form. Introduce **Diálogo** 4 at the end of Section 10, "Talking About Yourself."

* **tú** means *you* in Spanish; **tú** is used when you are speaking to a close relative, a friend, or a child — someone with whom you are familiar. To say *you*, the Spanish also use **usted** when speaking to a stranger or a grown-up — a person with whom you should be formal. The exercises in this book use **tú** and its related form **te**.

Now let's review what you learned in Dialog 1:

1. Buenos días, _____ (name).

   Buenos días, _____ (name).

2. ¿Cómo te llamas?

   Me llamo _____ .

3. Mucho gusto, _____ (name).

   El gusto es mío, _____ (name).

4. Adiós.
   Adiós.

Rincón cultural

Spanish Names

Hispanic children are very lucky: they celebrate not only their birthday but also their name day, known in Spanish as **el Día del Santo** because most Spanish names come from the names of saints. If you look at a Spanish calendar you will notice that each day is devoted to a different saint. On their name day, Hispanic children may receive presents and celebrate at a party with relatives and friends. Everyone wishes them **¡Feliz día de tu santo!** *(Happy Name Day!)*

Spanish names are, of course, different from American names. Each person has two family names: the father's last name followed by the mother's maiden name. For example, if a girl's full name is **Ana Gómez Álvarez**, it means that her father's last

NOTE TO TEACHERS

➡ Introduce the words **señor, señora, señorita** on the chalkboard by writing the words before names of people students know. Model pronunciation for the class.

➡ Greet students and ask them to respond by greeting you with **"Buenos días, señor (señora, señorita)."**

➡ Tell students your name, then ask theirs. Have students ask their classmates their names.

Have students take turns greeting one another.

➡ Circulate among students, shaking hands with them as you say, **"Mucho gusto, señor (señorita) _____(last name)"**; and they reply, **"El gusto es mío, señor (señora) _____ (your name)."** They could then proceed to shake hands with each other.

➡ Explain to students that whenever the Spanish greet someone whose name they do not know, the greeting is generally followed by **señor, señora,** or **señorita.** For example, when entering a shop, say, **"Buenos días, señora"** to a female clerk. When leaving, say, **"Adiós, señora."**

➡ In pairs, have students practice the entire dialog. Challenge students to improvise a skit in front of the class between two people who have just met, ending with **"Adiós, señor (señora, señorita)."**

NOTE TO TEACHERS

➡ You may wish to help students find their names or family members' names on the name day calendar. Ask students to find a friend or an acquaintance whom they can wish **¡Feliz día de tu santo!**

➡ If the class includes students from different ethnic backgrounds, ask them if their families celebrate name days.

➡ Point out that compound names like **Ana María, María Luisa, José Luis,** and **Juan Carlos** are very common Spanish names. Ask students if compound names are popular in the United States and if they can think of a few examples, such as Anne Marie, Billy Joe, Betty Jane, Norma Jean, Peggy Sue.

ENERO

1	María Madre de D.
2	S. Gregorio N.
3	Sta. Genoveva
4	Sta. Mónica
5	S. Eufrasio
6	**EPIFANÍA**
7	S. Raimundo de P.
8	S. Severino
9	S. Julián
10	S. Nicanor
11	S. Martín de L.
12	Sta. Tatiana
13	S. Hilario
14	S. Fulgencio
15	S. Pablo p. e.
16	S. Marino
17	S. Antonio de E.
18	Sta. Vicenta
19	S. Mario
20	S. Sebastián
21	Sta. Inés
22	S. Vicente
23	S. Ildefonso
24	S. Francisco de S.
25	Conv. de S. Pablo
26	S. Timoteo
27	Sta. Angela de M.
28	Sto. Tomás de A.
29	S. Pedro N.
30	S. Lesmes
31	S. Juan Bosco

FEBRERO

1	Sta. Brígida
2	**Pres. del Señor**
3	S. Oscar
4	S. Juan de B.
5	Sta. Águeda
6	S. Pablo Miki
7	S. Romualdo
8	S. Jerónimo E.
9	Sta. Apolonia
10	Sta. Escolástica
11	Sra. de Lourdes
12	Sta. Eulalia
13	S. Benigno
14	S. Metodio
15	S. Claudio
16	S. Onésimo
17	Siete Santos
18	S. Eladio
19	S. Conrado
20	Sta. Amanda
21	S. Pedro D.
22	S. Pedro
23	S. Policarpo
24	S. Modesto
25	S. Cesáreo
26	S. Alejandro
27	S. Leandro
28	S. Gabriel de D.

MARZO

1	S. Albino
2	S. Heraclio
3	S. Juan de D.
4	S. Casimiro
5	S. Adrián
6	S. Olegario
7	Sta. Felícitas
8	S. Juan
9	Sta. Francisca R.
10	S. Cavo
11	S. Eulogio
12	S. Gregorio M.
13	S. Rodrigo
14	Sta. Matilde
15	S. Raimundo de F.
16	S. Ciriaco
17	S. Patricio
18	S. Cirilo de J.
19	S. José
20	S. Martín de D.
21	S. Alfonso de R.
22	S. Bienvenido
23	S. Toribio de M.
24	S. Agapito
25	**ANUNCIACIÓN**
26	S. Braulio
27	S. Ruperto
28	Sta. Gundelina
29	Sta. Beatriz de S.
30	S. Juan Cl.
31	S. Benjamín

ABRIL

1	S. Hugo
2	S. Francisco de P.
3	S. Ricardo
4	S. Isodoro
5	S. Vicente F.
6	Sta. Juliana
7	S. Juan Bautista
8	S. Dionisio
9	Sta. Casilda
10	S. Miguel de los S.
11	S. Estanislao
12	S. Víctor
13	S. Martín I.
14	S. Tiburcio
15	S. Telmo
16	Sta. Engracia
17	Sta. Clara
18	S. Perfecto
19	S. Hermógenes
20	S. Teodoro
21	S. Anselmo
22	S. Lucio
23	S. Jorge
24	S. Fidel
25	S. Marcos
26	Ntra. Sra. del B.
27	Sta. Zita
28	S. Pedro Ch.
29	Sta. Catalina de S.
30	S. Pío V.

MAYO

1	S. José O.
2	S. Atanasio
3	S. Felipe
4	S. Silvano
5	S. Máximo
6	S. Heliodoro
7	Sta. Flavia
8	S. Víctor
9	S. Gregorio O.
10	San Juan de A.
11	S. Francisco J.
12	S. Nereo
13	S. Miguel G.
14	S. Matías
15	S. Isidro
16	Sta. Felicia
17	S. Pascual
18	S. Juan I.
19	S. Juan de C.
20	S. Bernardino
21	S. Andrés B.
22	Sta. Rita
23	S. Desiderio
24	**María Auxiliadora**
25	S. Gregorio VII
26	S. Felipe N.
27	S. Agustín de C.
28	S. Justo
29	S. Félix
30	S. Fernando
31	**Visit. de la Virgen**

JUNIO

1	S. Justino
2	S. Marcelino
3	S. Carlos L.
4	S. Francisco
5	S. Bonifacio
6	S. Norberto
7	S. Pedro de C.
8	S. Eutropio
9	S. Efrén
10	S. Aresio
11	S. Bernabé
12	S. Juan de S.
13	S. Antonio de P.
14	S. Basilio
15	Sta. Benilde
16	S. Juan F.
17	Sta. Sancha
18	S. Venancio
19	Sta. Juliana
20	Sta. Florentina
21	S. Luis G.
22	S. Paulino
23	S. Áñigo
24	Nat. S. Juan B.
25	S. Guillermo
26	S. Marciano
27	S. Cirilo de A.
28	S. Ireneo
29	S. Pedro y Pablo
30	S. Marcial

JULIO

1	S. Simeón
2	S. Vidal
3	Sto. Tomás
4	Sta. Isabel de P.
5	S. Antonio M. Z.
6	Sta. María G.
7	S. Fermín
8	S. Edgar
9	Sta. Verónica
10	S. Honorato
11	S. Benito
12	S. Juan G.
13	S. Enrique
14	S. Camilo
15	S. Buenaventura
16	Ntra. Sra. del Carmen
17	S. Mártires del B.
18	S. Federico
19	Sta. Áurea
20	S. Pablo de C.
21	S. Lorenzo
22	Sta. María Magd.
23	Sta. Brígida
24	S. Francisco S.
25	S. Santiago
26	S. Joaquín
27	S. Aurelio
28	S. Gerardino
29	Sta. Marta
30	S. Pedro Cr.
31	S. Ignacio de L.

AGOSTO

1	S. Alfonso M.
2	S. Eusebio
3	S. Lidia
4	S. Juan María
5	Sta. María la Mayor
6	Transf. del Señor
7	Sto. Domingo
8	S. Cayetano
9	S. Marcelino
10	S. Lorenzo
11	Sta. Clara
12	S. Graciliano
13	S. Ponciano
14	S. Ursicio
15	**ASUNCIÓN**
16	S. Esteban de H.
17	S. Jacinto
18	Sta. Elena
19	S. Juan E.
20	S. Bernardo
21	S. Pío X
22	Sta. María Reina
23	Sta. Rosa
24	S. Bartolomé
25	S. Luis de Fr.
26	Sta. María Micaela
27	Sta. Mónica
28	S. Agustín
29	S. Juan Bautista
30	S. Esteban de Z.
31	S. Ramón

SEPTIEMBRE

1	S. Gil
2	S. Antolín
3	S. Gregorio
4	Sta. Cándida
5	S. Sancho
6	S. Juan de R.
7	Sta. Regina
8	**Nativ. de María**
9	S. Pedro C.
10	S. Nicolás de T.
11	Sta. Teodora
12	S. Leoncio
13	S. Juan Cr.
14	**Exaltac. Santa Cruz**
15	Virgen de los Dolor.
16	S. Cornelio
17	S. Roberto
18	S. José de C.
19	S. Jenaro
20	Sta. Imelda
21	S. Mateo
22	S. Mauricio
23	S. Constancio
24	Sta. Mercedes
25	S. Cleofás
26	S. Damián
27	S. Daniel
28	S. Wenceslao
29	S. Rafael
30	S. Jerónimo

OCTUBRE

1	Sta. Teresita
2	S. Angeles C.
3	S. Virilio
4	S. Francisco de A.
5	S. Froilán
6	S. Bruno
7	Ntra. Sra. del Ros.
8	S. Juan de Jesus
9	S. Luis B.
10	Ntra. Sra. del Pil.
11	Sta. Soledad
12	S. Serafín
13	S. Eduardo
14	S. Calixto
15	Sta. Teresa
16	Sta. Margarita de A.
17	S. Ignacio de A.
18	S. Lucas
19	S. Pedro de A.
20	Sta. Irene
21	S. Hilarión
22	Sta. Nunila
23	S. Juan de C.
24	S. Antonio
25	S. Crisanto
26	S. Felicísimo
27	S. Florencio
28	S. Simón
29	S. Narciso
30	S. Alonso
31	S. Quintín

NOVIEMBRE

1	**Todos los Santos**
2	**Fieles Difuntos**
3	S. Martín de P.
4	S. Carlos B.
5	S. Galación
6	S. Leonardo
7	S. Amaranto
8	S. Godofeo
9	S. Alejandro
10	S. León
11	S. José K.
12	Cuatro Santos
13	S. Eugenio
14	S. Gerardo
15	Sta. Eugenia
16	Sta. Gertrudis
17	Sta. Isabel de H.
18	S. Pedro y Pablo
19	S. Crispín
20	S. Félix de V.
21	**Pres. de la Virgen**
22	Sta. Cecilia
23	S. Clemente
24	Sta. Flora
25	S. Erasmo
26	S. Leonardo
27	S. Alberto
28	S. Jaime
29	S. Saturnino
30	S. Andrés

DICIEMBRE

1	S. Eloy
2	Sta. Bibiana
3	S. Francisco J.
4	S. Juan D.
5	S. Humberto
6	S. Nicolás
7	S. Ambrosio
8	**Imm. Concepción**
9	Sta. Valeria
10	Imm. Concepción Eulalia
11	S. Daniel
12	Sta. Juana F.
13	Sta. Lucía
14	S. Juan de la C.
15	Sta. Silvia
16	S. Adón
17	S. Roque
18	Sta. Esperanza
19	S. Nemesio
20	S. Julio
21	S. Pedro C.
22	S. Demetrio
23	Sta. Victoria
24	S. Delfín
25	**NATIVIDAD**
26	S. Esteban
27	S. Juan E.
28	Stos. Inocentes
29	Sto. Tomás B.
30	S. Rainerio
31	S. Silvestre

name is **Gómez**, and her mother's maiden name is **Álvarez**. If **Ana** marries **Carlos Pérez Fernández,** their child's last names will be **Pérez Gómez**. **Ana** herself would be **Señora Ana Gómez Álvarez de Pérez**, because women in the Hispanic world keep their maiden name after marriage. Sounds complicated? It really isn't, once you get used to it!

With the help of your teacher, find out what your name and your mother's name would be if you lived in a Spanish-speaking country.

4 Numbers

Conchita's clues:

$$\left.\begin{array}{l} c+e \\ c+i \end{array}\right\} = c \text{ in cent}$$

$$\left.\begin{array}{l} c+a \\ c+o \\ c+u \end{array}\right\} = c \text{ in cat}$$

cator**c**e, **c**inco

cator**c**e, **C**onchita, **c**uatro

You will soon be able to count to forty in Spanish. Listen to your teacher or the cassette to learn how to say the numbers 1 to 20.

1 uno 2 dos 3 tres 4 cuatro 5 cinco 6 seis
7 siete 8 ocho 9 nueve 10 diez 11 once 12 doce 13 trece
14 catorce 15 quince 16 diez y seis 17 diez y siete 18 diez y ocho 19 diez y nueve 20 veinte

➡ *Conchita's clues:* Model pronunciation of the Spanish **ce, ci,** and **ca, co, cu** sounds for students. For additional practice words, refer to the list of cognates on pages 10 and 11, or the list of names on page 13.

➡ Model pronunciation of numbers 1 to 10 or have students listen to the cassette, allowing time for repetition.

➡ Have students repeat groups of numbers:

- ◆ **uno, dos, tres / cuatro, cinco, seis / siete, ocho, nueve, diez**
- ◆ **uno, dos, tres, cuatro, cinco / seis, siete, ocho, nueve, diez**
- ◆ **diez, nueve, ocho, siete, seis, cinco, cuatro, tres, dos, uno**
- ◆ **dos, cuatro, seis, ocho, diez / uno, tres, cinco, siete, nueve**

➡ **¿Cuántos?** = *How many?* Hold up one finger, then two, then three, and so on. Each time, ask, **"¿Cuántos?"** allowing the whole class time to respond.

➡ Model pronunciation of numbers 11 to 20 or have students listen to the cassette, allowing time for repetition.

➡ Have students repeat these numbers in groups, as above.

➡ Count from **uno** to **veinte** with even numbers, then with odd.

➡ As a listening comprehension activity, have each student write his or her telephone number, real or made up, on a piece of paper. Students then drop the telephone numbers into a box. Choose a student to pick a number from the box and read it aloud in Spanish to the class. As soon as the telephone number is recognized, the student yells out: **"¡Es mío!"** (*"It's mine!"*). That student then picks another number from the box and reads it aloud to the class.

➡ Indicate people and objects in the classroom: the teacher, light(s), desk, books on the desk, doors, windows, pencils, girls, boys. After pointing to a person or object or to a group of people or objects, query, **"¿Cuántos?"**

NOTE TO TEACHERS

➡ As a vocabulary study aid for students, you may wish to duplicate the format of this first **Actividad** in each of the sections that follow. List Spanish words to be learned in the left column followed by blank rules. List English equivalents in the right column. Illustrations may substitute English equivalents.

➡ In the second **Actividad,** have students write the numbers they hear, stopping after every four numbers to check answers.

ANSWERS TO ACTIVIDAD *(teacher dictation in brackets)*

1. [ocho]	**8**	**5.** [trece]	**13**	**9.** [seis]	**6**
2. [veinte]	**20**	**6.** [diez y siete]	**17**	**10.** [diez y nueve]	**19**
3. [dos]	**2**	**7.** [catorce]	**14**	**11.** [quince]	**15**
4. [diez y ocho]	**18**	**8.** [doce]	**12**	**12.** [once]	**11**

➡ Here is a song to practice numbers. Have students make gestures to accompany the numbers and the action verbs. You may also adapt this song to practice numbers 11 to 40.

Números

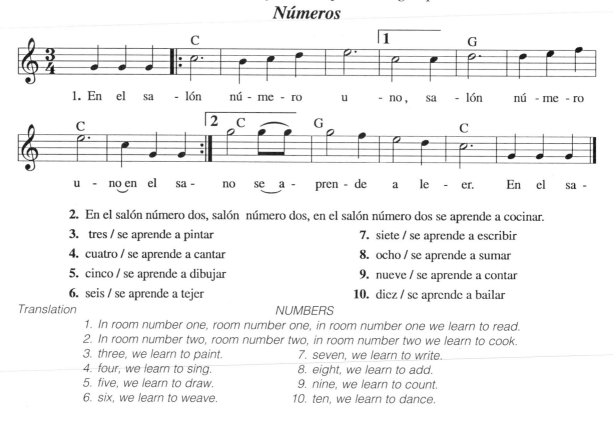

2. En el salón número dos, salón número dos, en el salón número dos se aprende a cocinar.

3. tres / se aprende a pintar

4. cuatro / se aprende a cantar

5. cinco / se aprende a dibujar

6. seis / se aprende a tejer

7. siete / se aprende a escribir

8. ocho / se aprende a sumar

9. nueve / se aprende a contar

10. diez / se aprende a bailar

Translation   *NUMBERS*

1. In room number one, room number one, in room number one we learn to read.

2. In room number two, room number two, in room number two we learn to cook.

3. three, we learn to paint.   *7. seven, we learn to write.*

4. four, we learn to sing.   *8. eight, we learn to add.*

5. five, we learn to draw.   *9. nine, we learn to count.*

6. six, we learn to weave.   *10. ten, we learn to dance.*

1. Cover page 18 with a sheet of paper. Then cover the Spanish number words below and say the numbers aloud in Spanish.
2. Now cover the Spanish number words and write the Spanish number words in the blank lines.

catorce	_____	14	diez	_____	10
cinco	_____	5	dos	_____	2
ocho	_____	8	veinte	_____	20
diez y nueve	_____	19	seis	_____	6
doce	_____	12	once	_____	11
diez y ocho	_____	18	tres	_____	3
nueve	_____	9	quince	_____	15
diez y seis	_____	16	siete	_____	7
cuatro	_____	4	trece	_____	13
diez y siete	_____	17	uno	_____	1

3. Pretend you are the teacher and correct your work with a red pen or pencil. You will be able to see at a glance which words you need to study further.

ACTIVIDAD

Your teacher will read some Spanish numbers to you. Write the numerals for the number you hear:

1. _____   4. _____   7. _____   10. _____

2. _____   5. _____   8. _____   11. _____

3. _____   6. _____   9. _____   12. _____

Let's continue learning numbers. Listen to your teacher or the cassette to learn how to say the numbers 21 to 40.

21 veinte y uno
22 veinte y dos
23 veinte y tres
24 veinte y cuatro
25 veinte y cinco
26 veinte y seis
27 veinte y siete
28 veinte y ocho
29 veinte y nueve
30 treinta
31 treinta y uno
32 treinta y dos
33 treinta y tres
34 treinta y cuatro
35 treinta y cinco
36 treinta y seis
37 treinta y siete
38 treinta y ocho
39 treinta y nueve
40 cuarenta

ACTIVIDAD

Cover the top of page 20 with a sheet of paper while you do the next three activities. Your teacher will read some numbers from 21 to 40 in random order to you. Write the numerals for the Spanish number you hear:

1. _____   6. _____

2. _____   7. _____

3. _____   8. _____

4. _____   9. _____

5. _____   10. _____

Note to Teachers

➡ Model pronunciation of numbers 21 to 30 or have students listen to the cassette, allowing time for repetition.

➡ Ask students if they see a pattern in the numbers 21 to 30. After they point out the pattern, ask them to try to compose the numbers 31 to 39 aloud.

➡ Now model pronunciation of numbers 31 to 40 or have students listen to the cassette, allowing time for repetition.

➡ Have students repeat groups of numbers sequentially—even and odd, forward and then backward.

➡ Have students repeat numbers 20 to 40 in multiples of 2 and 5, forward and then backward.

➡ For additional review, write a number on a piece of paper for each student in the class. Distribute numbers at random. Without recourse to the piece of paper, students say their numbers to their classmates in order to line up in the correct number order. Once lined up, have students yell out their numbers in sequence.

➡ For authentic practice in writing number words, distribute copies of blank checks with a dollar amount written in digits. Have students complete the checks by writing the dollar amount from 1 to 40 in words.

➡ Have students write the numbers they hear, stopping after every five numbers to check answers.

ANSWERS TO ACTIVIDAD *(teacher dictation in brackets)*

1. [veinte]   *20*
2. [veinte y cuatro] *24*
3. [treinta y seis]   *36*
4. [treinta y cinco] *35*
5. [treinta y uno]   *31*

6. [veinte y ocho] *28*
7. [treinta]   *30*
8. [veinte y uno]   *21*
9. [treinta y tres] *33*
10. [cuarenta]   *40*

ANSWERS TO ACTIVIDAD

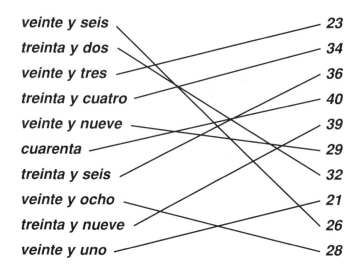

veinte y seis	23
treinta y dos	34
veinte y tres	36
treinta y cuatro	40
veinte y nueve	39
cuarenta	29
treinta y seis	32
veinte y ocho	21
treinta y nueve	26
veinte y uno	28

➡ Have students write the Spanish number words for the numbers they hear, stopping after every five numbers to check answers.

ANSWERS TO ACTIVIDAD *(teacher dictation in brackets)*

1. [thirty-two]   *treinta y dos*
2. [twenty-three]   *veinte y tres*
3. [thirty-seven]   *treinta y siete*
4. [twenty-nine]   *veinte y nueve*
5. [twenty-six]   *veinte y seis*

6. [thirty-four]   *treinta y cuatro*
7. [thirty-eight]   *treinta y ocho*
8. [twenty-two]   *veinte y dos*
9. [thirty-nine]   *treinta y nueve*
10. [twenty-five]   *veinte y cinco*

See how many Spanish number words you can recognize. Draw a line to match the Spanish number word with its numeral:

veinte y seis	23
treinta y dos	34
veinte y tres	36
treinta y cuatro	40
veinte y nueve	39
cuarenta	29
treinta y seis	32
veinte y ocho	21
treinta y nueve	26
veinte y uno	28

Now your teacher will read some numbers in English. Write the number words in Spanish:

1. _____   6. _____

2. _____   7. _____

3. _____   8. _____

4. _____   9. _____

5. _____   10. _____

Now that you know the numbers from 1 to 40, let's try some math. First let's look at some words you will need to know:

cinco **y** ocho **son** trece

diez y nueve menos siete son doce

$5 + 8 = 13$ $19 - 7 = 12$

Now write the answers to the following arithmetic problems in Spanish. Then find the correct answers in the puzzle. Circle them from left to right, right to left, up or down, or diagonally:

1. cuatro y cinco son _____

2. once y diez y siete son _____

3. veinte y cinco y catorce son _____

4. doce y tres son _____

5. siete y seis son _____

6. treinta y ocho menos veinte y dos son _____

7. trece y catorce son _____

8. treinta y dos menos veinte y cinco son _____

9. veinte y ocho menos diez y seis son _____

10. diez y nueve menos cinco son _____

11. nueve menos seis son _____

12. cuarenta menos cinco son _____

NOTE TO TEACHERS

➡ If this **Actividad** is done in class, check answers to math problems before students begin the word search.

➡ Tell students that accents on capital letters may be omitted for this and all other puzzles in the book.

ANSWERS TO ACTIVIDAD

1. *nueve*
2. *veinte y ocho*
3. *treinta y nueve*
4. *quince*
5. *trece*
6. *diez y seis*
7. *veinte y siete*
8. *siete*
9. *doce*
10. *catorce*
11. *tres*
12. *treinta y cinco*

ANSWERS TO ACTIVIDAD *(continued)*

13. *cinco*
14. *veinte*
15. *cuarenta*
16. *treinta*
17. *diez y siete*
18. *veinte y dos*
19. *diez y nueve*
20. *once*

13. siete menos dos son _____

14. diez y diez son _____

15. treinta y tres y siete son _____

16. veinte y tres y siete son _____

17. quince y dos son _____

18. treinta y siete menos quince son _____

19. quince y cuatro son _____

20. diez y uno son _____

```
D I E Z Y S E I S A S P L S T
A O C N I C Y A T N I E R T S
E V E I N T E Y O C H O R I E
T E Y O D I R S M E Z R E T V
E R A E C N O E T C S T I S E
I O T Q A D X N C X E S P S U
S C N H G I I N D E P Z U A N
Y N E Z V E I N T E Y D O S Y
E I R E V Z S A T N I E R T A
T C A C Z Y E Z Y B U R E E T
N T U R Z S L P C S Q R D V N
I Q C O D I E Z Y N U E V E I
E R C T N E R O G Q R T O U E
V O C A U T R A E A N E U N R
T D O C E E S I E C N I U Q T
```

5 Days of the Week

Conchita's clues:

$g+i \begin{cases} j \\ g+e \end{cases} =h$ in hurry

jueves, Jaime, Gilberto, generación

NOVIEMBRE

lunes	martes	miércoles	jueves	viernes	sábado	domingo
1	2	3	4	5	6	7
8	9	10	11	12	13	14
15	16	17	18	19	20	21
22	23	24	25	26	27	28
29	30	31				

These are the days of the week in Spanish. The first letter is not capitalized. The Spanish week begins with Monday.

Hoy es lunes. = *Today is Monday.*

Each day, find as many people as you can and tell them the day of the week in Spanish.

NOTE TO TEACHERS

➡ *Conchita's clues:* Model pronunciation of the Spanish **j, gi,** and **ge** sounds for students.

➡ After drilling the days of the week with a wall calendar or calendar transparency, have students take turns greeting the class with, **"Buenos días, clase. Hoy es _____."**

➡ At the beginning of each class period, have a different student greet the class, say the day of the week, and write it on the chalkboard.

➡ Here is a song students can enjoy while practicing the days of the week.

Los días de la semana

1. Lu - nes, lu - nes, lu — nes em - pie- zan las cla - ses en mi es - cue — la.

2. Martes, martes, martes segundo día de mis clases.

3. Miércoles, miércoles, miércoles seguimos las clases en mi escuela.

4. Jueves, jueves, jueves todos vamos para el parque.

5. Viernes, viernes, viernes cambiamos de asiento en mi clase.

6. Sábado, sábado, sábado limpiamos los muebles en mi casa.

7. Domingo, domingo, domingo jugamos con nuestros amigos.

Translation

DAYS OF THE WEEK

1. Monday, Monday, Monday classes begin at my school.
2. Tuesday, Tuesday, Tuesday second day of my classes.
3. Wednesday, Wednesday, Wednesday continue my classes at school.
4. Thursday, Thursday, Thursday we all go to the park.
5. Friday, Friday, Friday we change seats in my class.
6. Saturday, Saturday, Saturday we clean the furniture in my house.
7. Sunday, Sunday, Sunday we play with our friends.

Rincón cultural (Supplementary Culture)

Students may be interested in comparing Spanish and American school systems.

➡ Schools in most Spanish-speaking countries consist of the following levels:

- **Primary School**
  Nursery school and kindergarten: children two to five years old
  Elementary school, grades 1 to 6: students six to eleven years old

- **Secondary School**
  Most students attend five to six years of secondary school. According to students' academic performance in elementary school, they may attend a vocational high school to learn a trade, an **escuela normal** to become teachers, or a **colegio** to prepare for university studies.

Rincón cultural En la escuela (At school)

Complete the following school schedule with the subjects you are taking this year:

	LUNES	MARTES	MIERCOLES	JUEVES	VIERNES

Now look at a schedule of a Mexican middle-school student. Compare it with yours. What are the differences? What are the similarities?

	LUNES	MARTES	MIERCOLES	JUEVES	VIERNES
7:00 – 7:50	Math	Math	Math	Math	Math
8:00 – 8:50	English	English	English	English	English
9:00 – 9:50	Science	Science	Science	Science	Science
10:00 – 10:50	Social Studies	Social Studies	Social Studies	Social Studies	Social Studies
11:00 – 11:50	Spanish	Spanish	Spanish	Spanish	Spanish
1:00 – 1:50	Physical Education	Physical Education	Physical Education	Physical Education	Physical Education

As you can see, this Mexican student's school day begins and ends early. In some urban areas, where the population is very high, two school shifts exist: from 7:00 a.m. to 2:00 p.m. and from 2:00 p.m. to 8:00 p.m. In many cities, a third school shift is available for adults.

Although grading systems vary in Spanish-speaking countries, often a 10-point grading system is used — 10 being the highest grade, 1 the lowest, and 5 the passing grade. In Mexico and Puerto Rico, students' grades range from 0 to 100.

6 Months of the Year

Conchita's clues:

$$g+a$$
$$g+o$$
$$g+u$$
$= g$ in gust

Margarita, agosto, gusto

The months of the year in Spanish resemble English.
Can you recognize all of them?

ENERO

FEBRERO

MARZO

ABRIL

MAYO

JUNIO

JULIO

AGOSTO

SEPTIEMBRE

OCTUBRE

NOVIEMBRE

DICIEMBRE

➡ *Conchita's clues:* Model pronunciation of the Spanish **ga, go,** and **gu** sounds for students. Additional practice words may include: **gas, Gabriel, gorila, domingo, Guatemala.**

➡ You may wish to use a wall calendar or transparency to introduce the names of the months.

Drill the months by going up and down the rows, eliciting the names of the months sequentially **enero** to **diciembre** and then backward **diciembre** to **enero.** As students gain confidence, pick up speed.

ANSWERS TO ACTIVIDAD

1. A G O S T O

2. J U L I O

3. O C T U B R E

4. E N E R O

5. M A Y O

6. S E P T I E M B R E

7. M A R Z O

8. J U N I O

9. N O V I E M B R E

10. D I C I E M B R E

11. F E B R E R O

12. A B R I L

Unscramble the letters to form the name of a Spanish month:

1. T G O A O S

2. L O U I J

3. R E U C T B O

4. N E O R E

5. O M Y A

6. E M B P T S R E I E

7. Z A R M O

8. N I O U J

9. N E B M I O R E V

10. E D M R C E I I B

11. R E R F B O E

12. L I B R A

Match the names of the months with their numbers by drawing lines between the two columns. For example, January is number one and December is number twelve:

abril	nueve
agosto	dos
diciembre	diez
enero	cuatro
febrero	seis
julio	tres
junio	once
marzo	siete
mayo	uno
noviembre	ocho
octubre	doce
septiembre	cinco

ANSWERS TO ACTIVIDAD

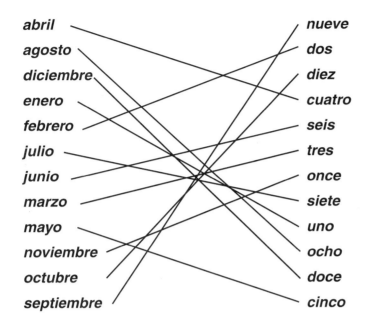

abril	nueve
agosto	dos
diciembre	diez
enero	cuatro
febrero	seis
julio	tres
junio	once
marzo	siete
mayo	uno
noviembre	ocho
octubre	doce
septiembre	cinco

NOTE TO TEACHERS

➡   To practice the months of the year, students may enjoy saying a Spanish version of the familiar "Thirty Days Has November."

Treinta días hay en noviembre, y en abril, junio y septiembre.
De veinte y ocho sólo hay uno, los demás de treinta y uno.

Thirty days has November, April, June, and September.
Of twenty-eight there's only one, all the rest have thirty-one.

Answers to Actividad will vary.

➡ Here is a song students will enjoy to practice the months of the year.

Meses del año

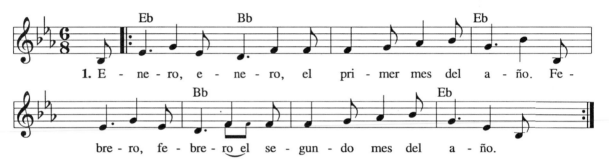

1. E - ne - ro, e - ne - ro, el pri - mer mes del a - ño. Fe - bre - ro, fe - bre - ro el se - gun - do mes del a - ño.

2. Marzo, marzo, el tercer mes del año.
Abril, abril, el cuarto mes del año.

3. Mayo, mayo, el quinto mes del año.
Junio, junio, el sexto mes del año.

4. Julio, julio, el séptimo mes del año.
Agosto, agosto, el octavo mes del año.

5. Septiembre, septiembre, el noveno mes del año.
Octubre, octubre, el décimo mes del año.

6. Noviembre, noviembre, el undécimo mes del año.
Diciembre, diciembre, el duodécimo mes del año.

Translation

MONTHS OF THE YEAR

1. *January, January, the first month of the year.*
February, February, the second month of the year.

2. *March, March, the third month of the year.*
April, April, the fourth month of the year.

3. *May / fifth*
June / sixth

4. *July / seventh*
August / eight

5. *September / ninth*
October / tenth

6. *November / eleventh*
December / twelfth

Answer the following questions with the Spanish months:

1. In which months do you have vacation?

_____

2. In which month is your birthday?

_____

3. In which month does your mother celebrate her birthday?

_____

4. In which month does your father celebrate his birthday?

_____

5. In which month does your best friend celebrate her/his

birthday? _____

6. When does your teacher celebrate her/his birthday?

_____

7. Which is your favorite month?

_____

8. Which is your least favorite month?

_____

Fill in the blanks with the correct Spanish names of the days or months, then find the nineteen names of the day or month in the puzzle. Circle them from left to right, right to left, up or down, or diagonally:

1. The day after Monday: _____

2. The day before Thursday: _____

3. The last day of your school week: _____

4. The day before Friday: _____

5. The first day of the weekend: _____

6. Many people go to church on this day of the week: _____

7. The first day of your school week: _____

8. The month of the United States' birthday: _____

9. Labor Day occurs toward the beginning of this month: _____

10. New Year's day is the first day of this month: _____

11. April Fool's Day is the first day of this month: _____

12. The month of Christmas: _____

13. Memorial Day occurs toward the end of this month: _____

14. The month of Valentine's Day: _____

15. The month after July: _____

ANSWERS TO ACTIVIDAD

1. *martes*
2. *miércoles*
3. *viernes*
4. *jueves*
5. *sábado*
6. *domingo*
7. *lunes*
8. *julio*
9. *septiembre*
10. *enero*
11. *abril*
12. *diciembre*
13. *mayo*
14. *febrero*
15. *agosto*

ANSWERS TO ACTIVIDAD (continued)

16. *noviembre*

17. *octubre*

18. *marzo*

19. *junio*

16. The month of presidential elections: _____

17. Halloween is on the last day of this month: _____

18. The month of St. Patrick's day: _____

19. The first month of summer: _____

```
O D A B A S N U T U E S O O E
M M A R Z O H O N B E P I C A
I D A G O S T O V V A M L T Z
C I S E L O C R E I M X U U N
O Y V O Z O G U L V E G J B S
E A R S B P J D I A I M Y R E
R O U E N E R O R L B F B E P
B I T A X I E A T J H R O R T
M N V I E R N E S I A B I I E
E U P S Q P W O X M C T O L D
I J T O R E R B E F T I Y W A
C L N P D O M I N G O S A Q P
I E R B M E I T P E S J M K L
D O X P Q L U N E S E T R A M
```

Now that you have learned the names of the days and months, let's learn how to say dates. When Spanish speakers want to say, "Today is Friday, July fourteenth," they say, **"Hoy es viernes, el catorce de julio."** "Today is Friday, March first" would be **"Hoy es viernes, el primero* de marzo."**

Your teacher will now divide the class into small groups. Each of you will choose your birthday month and make up a calendar for that month. Complete the calendar with the days of the week and the month in Spanish and enter the dates.

LUNES						**DOMINGO**

Now that you have completed your calendar, take turns pointing to several dates and saying them to your partners. Then point to the date of your birthdate and say: **Mi cumpleaños es** (*My birthday is*) . . . followed by the date.

* Spanish uses the word **primero** instead of **uno** for the first day of the month.

NOTE TO TEACHERS

➡ Point to the classroom calendar or sketch one on the chalkboard. Point to a date and say, for example, **"Hoy es lunes, el ocho de octubre."** Call on students to identify other dates on the calendar.

➡ Now that students are able to say the date in Spanish, at the beginning of each class period, have a student greet the class, say the date, and write it on the chalkboard. The student says, for example, **"Buenos días, clase. Hoy es lunes, el ocho de octubre."**

➡ Divide the class into groups of three and have each student fill in the month, days, and dates of the blank calendars to reflect the month of his or her birthday this year. Group members then take turns choosing different dates and telling them to one another.

➡ Model **Mi cumpleaños es . . .** for students.

OCTUBRE						
LUNES	MARTES	MIÉRCOLES	JUEVES	VIERNES	SÁBADO	DOMINGO
		1	2	3	4	5
6	7	8	9	10	11	12
13	14	15	16	17	18	19
20	21	22	23	24	25	26
27	28	29	30	31		

NOTE TO TEACHERS

➡ *Conchita's clue:* Model pronunciation of the Spanish **y** sound for students.

➡ Linking **Diálogo** 2 and Section 7, "The Classroom"

Diálogo 2 and Section 7 will be most effective if treated as a unit. Students need to know the names of two or three classroom objects in order to do the activity that accompanies the dialog, and they need phrases and expressions of the dialog to discuss objects in the classroom. You could choose one or two additional objects for the activity, then use the new phrases students have just learned as they practice the vocabulary in Section 7.

➡ Before students are asked to read **Diálogo** 2 for meaning, have them look at the characters and guess what Elisa and Jaime may be saying to each other in each illustration.

➡ Explain that **una muchacha** means *a girl* and **una soda** means *a soda*.

➡ Next, model pronunciation either by reading aloud or by playing the cassette while students read the dialog.

➡ Have students close their books. Read short segments for students to repeat. If a phrase is too long, break it into shorter sections, reading the last part first.

➡ Ask questions such as:

- ◆ How does Elisa say "Hi"?
- ◆ How would she say "Good morning"?
- ◆ How does Elisa ask Jaime how he is?
- ◆ How does Jaime answer?
- ◆ Can you guess the difference between **"Estoy muy bien"** and **"Así, así"** by looking at the pictures? Explain that **Buenos días** means *Good morning* and **Hola** means *Hello* or *Hi*. Wait to introduce the distinction between formal and informal greetings until the following **Actividad.**

➡ Continue asking:

- ◆ What is Jaime drawing? What is it called in Spanish?
- ◆ What is Elisa holding? What is it called in Spanish?
- ◆ How does Jaime ask "What is this?"
- ◆ What does Elisa answer?
- ◆ How does Jaime say "Thank you"?
- ◆ How does Elisa say "You're welcome"?

Conchita's clue: **y** = ee of sheep

Y hoy, esto**y** mu**y** bien.

Now let's review what you learned in Dialog 2:

1. Hola, _____ (name of friend) ¿Cómo estás?

2. Así, así. ¿Y tú?
Estoy muy bien, gracias.

3. ¿Qué es?
Es un(a) _____.

4. Muchas gracias.
De nada.

Rincón cultural   Hispanic Holidays

What is the first thing many students look for on the school calendar? Days off. Students in Spanish-speaking countries are given time off for the following holidays:

All Saint's Day *(el Día de los Muertos):* November 1. A day of remembrance of relatives and friends who have passed on.

Christmas *(Navidad):* December 25. Christmas Eve is celebrated with a mass and a big dinner afterward. Many celebrate the season by singing late night serenades to relatives and friends, who in return offer them traditional food and drinks. Students enjoy two weeks of vacation during Christmas and New Year.

Epiphany *(el Día de los Reyes Magos):* January 6. This day commemorates the visit of the three kings bearing gifts to the infant Jesus. Most Hispanic children receive presents on January 6 instead of December 25.

NOTE TO TEACHERS

➡ Introduce the difference between formal and informal greetings in Spanish.

  ◆ Explain that when greeting a friend or classmate, you may say "**¡Hola!**" an informal way of saying *"Hi."*

  ◆ When greeting a teacher or an adult, say "**Buenos días, señor (señora, señorita).**"

➡ Greet several students with "**¡Hola, _____ (first name)!**" allowing them time to respond. Then have students greet you with "**Buenos días, señor (señorita) _____(last name).**"

➡ Have students practice greeting one another and asking "**¿Cómo estás . . . ?**" in small groups.

➡ Display a book and say, "**Es un libro.**" Have the class repeat. Then ask, "**¿Qué es?**" The class answers, "**Es un libro.**" Repeat the exercise with additional classroom items. Give students a chance to ask each other "**¿Qué es?**"

➡ Wait until Section 7, "The Classroom," to introduce gender of nouns. For now, explain that **un** and **una** mean *a, an* and that some words take **un** and others **una**.

➡ Continue asking "**¿Qué es?**" while pointing to other objects in the classroom. After each question and answer, say "**Muchas gracias.**" Instruct students to respond "**De nada.**" Have students practice in small groups with **¿Qué es?, Es un(a) _____ , Muchas gracias,** and **De nada.**

➡ Using hand puppets, have two students improvise a skit in front of the class between two people who meet, greet, ask each other to identify several objects in the classroom, and thank each other.

ANSWERS

1. *Generally, Hispanic children receive Christmas presents on the Epiphany, January 6.*

2. *The Spanish-speaking world celebrates the discovery of the New World and the richness of the Hispanic heritage.*

Rincón cultural (Supplementary Culture)

➡ Students may be interested in learning more about holidays and celebrations in Spanish-speaking countries. Here are some points for discussion.

- ◆ In Mexico, children celebrate their third birthday with a special church service in their honor called **la Presentación de los tres años.** At the age of 15, a girl is treated to a coming-out party or ball, where she is the center of attention.

- ◆ In Central and South America, the **piñata** is a favorite game played on Christmas and for birthdays. The **piñata** is a decorated vessel—a ceramic jar or a cardboard animal—filled with candies, fruits, and other goodies. It is hung from the ceiling, and blindfolded children take turns trying to break it with sticks and release its content. You may wish the class to celebrate Christmas or a student's birthday by making a **piñata** and playing at breaking it to the sounds of Hispanic music.

Good Friday *(Viernes Santo)* and **Easter** *(Pascua)* are two of the most important Hispanic holidays, when everyday life comes to a stop. People attend special masses, and thousands of devoted Christians participate in religious processions held in every city and town. Students enjoy a one-week recess during Easter.

Some of the following holidays are common to all or most Spanish-speaking countries, while others are individual to each country.

Columbus Day *(Día de la Raza):* October 12 is a holiday in the whole Spanish-speaking world. It commemorates the discovery of the New World. On this day, people celebrate the diversity, richness, and contributions of the races and cultures that make up the Hispanic identity.

Labor Day *(Día del Trabajo)* is celebrated on May 1, except in Puerto Rico, where the American tradition is followed.

Every Spanish American country has its own national holiday to commemorate important dates in its struggle for independence from Spain. For example, in Mexico, it's September 16; in Colombia, July 20; in Chile, September 18; in the Dominican Republic, February 27.

Each country also has holidays that commemorate other special historical events, such as May 5 in Mexico, which commemorates a victory against the French invasion in the nineteenth century, or November 19 in Puerto Rico, the day the island was discovered.

1. When do Hispanic children generally receive Christmas presents?

_____

2. What does the Spanish-speaking world celebrate on Columbus Day?

_____

7 The Classroom

Conchita's clues:

h is not pronounced in Spanish.

hola, hoy, hoja

qui=ki in ski
que=ka in skate

quince, ¿Qué es?

Learn the names of the objects in your classroom. See how many you can remember at a time without having to look at the book:

un estudiante
un muchacho

una silla

un cuaderno

una pluma

una mesa

un libro

NOTE TO TEACHERS

➡ *Conchita's clues:* Model pronunciation of the Spanish silent **h, qui,** and **que** sounds for students.

➡ Model pronunciation of classroom words or have students listen to the cassette, allowing time for repetition.

- ◆ Now point to a desk and say, **"Es un pupitre."** Have the class repeat.
- ◆ Indicate a piece of chalk: **"Es una tiza."**
- ◆ Silently point to the first object, allowing students time to recall and repeat its name.
- ◆ Name a third item, then have the class recall the names of previous objects.
- ◆ Continue adding items and repeating previously mentioned ones, stretching students' memories.

➡ Now is a good time to explain that Spanish nouns, or names of objects, are either masculine or feminine and that **un** is masculine and **una** is feminine. Some students may ask how to tell the gender of Spanish nouns. Explain that for some words it's easy. For example: **muchacha** and **profesora** are feminine, while **muchacho** and **profesor** are masculine. Although for other words, such as **un libro** (a book) or **una mesa** (a table), there is no logical explanation, there is a helpful hint: Words ending in **-o** are often masculine, and others ending in **-a** are often feminine. For nouns ending in other letters, suggest that students memorize the article along with each noun they learn.

➡ Use picture dictation for additional reinforcement. Have students draw the object they hear.

➡ A bingo game can easily be adapted as a listening comprehension activity for classroom objects. Draw ten objects on the chalkboard. Name the objects or have students name them. Ask students to pick five of the ten objects and draw them on a piece of paper. You then name the objects at random as students check if the objects are among those on their papers. The first student to cross out all five objects is the winner.

NOTE TO TEACHERS

Here is a song to practice classroom objects. Whenever possible have students make gestures to accompany the lyrics. You may wish students to continue singing with other classroom words:

La mesa es para poner.	*The table is for placing.*
La pluma es para anotar.	*The pen is for taking notes.*
El papel es para dibujar.	*The paper is for drawing.*
La pizarra es para mostrar.	*The chalkboard is for showing.*
La ventana es para abrir.	*The window is for opening.*

El salón de clases

2. El lápiz, el lápiz es para escribir.
   El lápiz, el lápiz es para escribir.

3. La silla, la silla es para sentar.
   La silla, la silla es para sentar.

4. La puerta, la puerta es para entrar.
   La puerta, la puerta es para entrar.

Translation

THE CLASSROOM

1. The book, the book is for reading.
   The book, the book is for reading.

2. The pencil, the pencil is for writing.
   The pencil, the pencil is for writing.

3. The chair, the chair is for sitting.
   The chair, the chair is for sitting.

4. The door, the door is for entering.
   The door, the door is for entering.

una pizarra

una ventana

una profesora

un pedazo de tiza

un profesor

una puerta   una hoja de papel

una estudiante
una muchacha

un pupitre

un lápiz

un escritorio

In Spanish, every noun is considered masculine or feminine. The masculine indefinite article *(a, an)* is **un** and the feminine is **una**.

ACTIVIDAD

1. Name aloud as many of the classroom words in Spanish as you can remember. Study the words you did not remember.

2. Write the name of the illustrations in Spanish in the first column of blank lines.

3. Correct your work. Give yourself one point for each correct answer.

4. Now cover the illustrations and write the English meanings of the Spanish words in the second column of blank lines.

5. Correct your work. Give yourself one point for each correct answer.

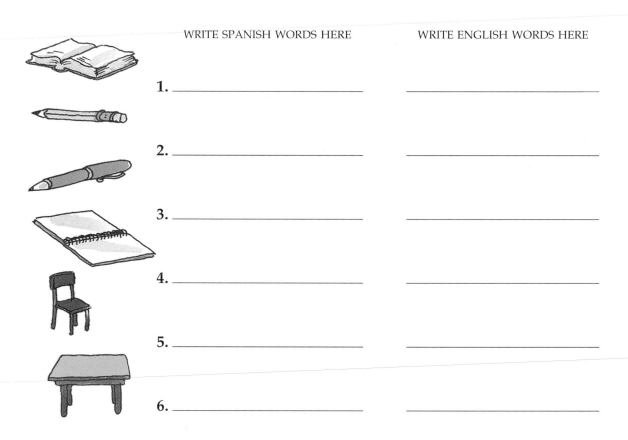

WRITE SPANISH WORDS HERE   WRITE ENGLISH WORDS HERE

1. _____   _____

2. _____   _____

3. _____   _____

4. _____   _____

5. _____   _____

6. _____   _____

This **Actividad** may be done in class or at home. If done in class, allow time for students to correct their work.

ANSWERS TO ACTIVIDAD

1. *un libro*   *a book*

2. *un lápiz*   *a pencil*

3. *una pluma*   *a pen*

4. *un cuaderno*   *a notebook*

5. *una silla*   *a chair*

6. *una mesa*   *a table*

ANSWERS TO ACTIVIDAD (continued)

7.	*una pizarra*	*a chalkboard*
8.	*un pedazo de tiza*	*a piece of chalk*
9.	*una puerta*	*a door*
10.	*una ventana*	*a window*
11.	*una hoja de papel*	*a sheet of paper*
12.	*un estudiante / un muchacho*	*a male student / a boy*
13.	*una estudiante / una muchacha*	*a female student / a girl*
14.	*un escritorio*	*a teacher's desk*
15.	*un pupitre*	*a student's desk*
16.	*un profesor*	*a male teacher*
17.	*una profesora*	*a female teacher*

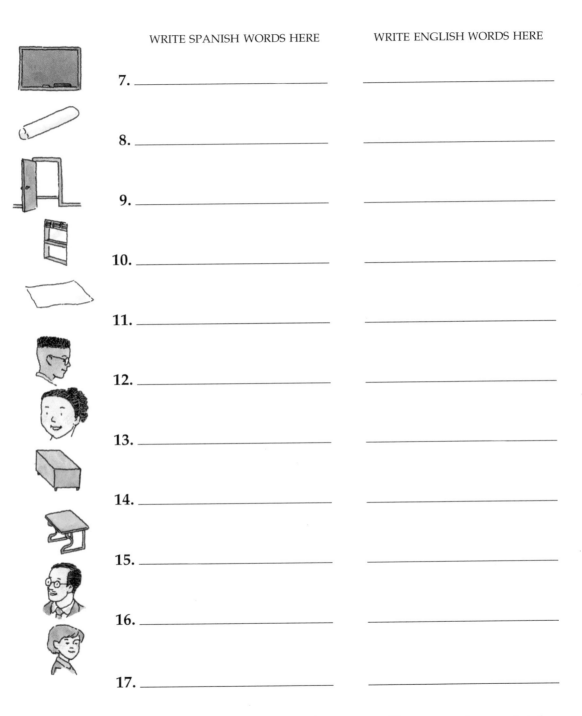

WRITE SPANISH WORDS HERE   WRITE ENGLISH WORDS HERE

7. _____   _____

8. _____   _____

9. _____   _____

10. _____   _____

11. _____   _____

12. _____   _____

13. _____   _____

14. _____   _____

15. _____   _____

16. _____   _____

17. _____   _____

Thirty-four points is a perfect score. If you made a mistake, you can improve your score by repeating the exercise on a blank piece of paper and correcting it again.

Classroom Vocabulary Puzzle: To solve this puzzle, first express the following words in Spanish then fit them in the puzzle vertically and horizontally:

4-letter words

table   — — — —

chalk   — — — —

5-letter words

book   — — — — —

paper   — — — — —

pencil   — — — — —

chair   — — — — —

pen   — — — — —

6-letter word

door   — — — — — —

7-letter words

chalkboard   — — — — — — —

window   — — — — — — —

8-letter words

boy   — — — — — — — —

girl   — — — — — — — —

notebook   — — — — — — — —

9-letter word

female teacher   — — — — — — — — —

ANSWERS TO ACTIVIDAD

4-letter words

table   **MESA**

chalk   **TIZA**

6-letter word

door   **PUERTA**

7-letter words

chalkboard   **PIZARRA**

window   **VENTANA**

8-letter words

boy   **MUCHACHO**

girl   **MUCHACHA**

notebook   **CUADERNO**

9-letter word

female teacher   **PROFESORA**

5-letter words

book   **LIBRO**

paper   **PAPEL**

pencil   **LÁPIZ**

chair   **SILLA**

pen   **PLUMA**

ANSWERS TO ACTIVIDAD

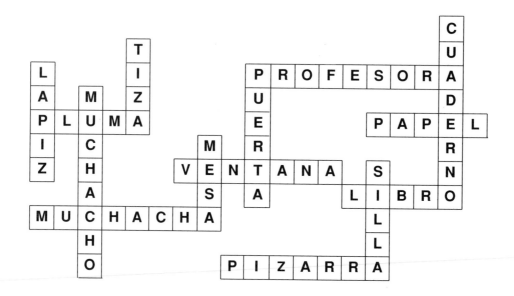

Rincón cultural Leisure Time

Hispanic children spend their free time in a variety of activities with family and friends. Because Hispanic schools normally do not sponsor activities like sports, dances, or games, most students go to youth centers or clubs to take classes in areas of interest ranging from music, dance, arts and crafts, to sports, martial arts, computer science, and foreign languages.

Hispanic teens like to go out in groups. Teenagers with similar backgrounds or from the same school tend to form a special group of close friends who meets regularly to chat at cafés, take walks, go dancing, and have parties. Even when teenagers date, usually beginning at the age of 16, it is still uncommon for a couple to go out alone unless the relationship is more serious.

In Hispanic cultures, life revolves around the family. Extended family members, including aunts, uncles, and cousins, enjoy close family ties and mutual support. A typical Hispanic family includes the parents, two or more children, one or two grandparents often living in the same home, and possibly an aunt or uncle. Grandparents have a very important role in family life: they contribute to raising the grandchildren, they share in the cooking and household duties, and their wisdom, opinions, and advice are very much respected and followed.

Meals are an important time for the family to gather, eat leisurely, and engage in lively conversation. Stores and offices generally close from noon to two o'clock in order to give workers time to go home and have a traditional midday meal with the family. If time allows, an afternoon siesta or nap is enjoyed before returning to work. The practice of extended midday breaks has been gradually disappearing in the large cities.

Does your family differ from the typical Hispanic family? How? _____

Answers may vary.

Rincón cultural (Supplementary Culture)

➡ Here are some additional culture notes on leisure time.

- Hispanic youngsters do many of the same things during their free time as their American counterparts. They watch television and videos, listen to music, and play video games. Youngsters spend much time with friends at one another's homes and often stay overnight on weekends. They also often study together.

- Young people in Spanish-speaking countries prefer going out in groups, and it is not unusual for as many as ten to twelve young people to arrange to go places together or plan parties and informal gatherings, usually in the afternoon.

- Since most teenagers do not own cars, friends like to take long walks in parks, in town squares, or main streets. They sing, joke, or chat at cafés. Young people also enjoy spending time with family and relatives. They often go out together to the movies, on outings in the country or the beach, on picnics, or simply for a Sunday stroll.

➡️ *Conchita's clues:* Model pronunciation of **ll, rr,** and **r** sounds for students. For additional practice, have students find similar words containing these sounds in vocabulary already learned: numbers, page 18; days of the week, page 24; months of the year, page 26; classroom objects, page 36; colors, page 43.

➡️ Model pronunciation of color words or have students listen to the cassette, allowing time for repetition. To teach colors, use crayons, paints, balloons, construction paper, and so on.

➡️ You may wish to use picture dictation as a listening comprehension activity. Have students draw and color the classroom objects they hear. For example, **un lápiz rojo, un libro azul, una pizarra verde.**

➡️ Here is a simple song to practice colors. You may wish to recycle classroom vocabulary by having students continue singing with additional classroom items: **el color de la pizarra, el color del cuaderno,** and so on.

Los colores

1. El co - lor de mi ban - de - ra, el co - lor de
mi ban - de - ra, el co - ra ro - jo, blan-co y a - zul.

2. El color del escritorio, el color del escritorio,
   el color del escritorio, morado y marrón.

3. El color del arco iris, el color del arco iris,
   el color del arco iris, rosado, verde y azul.

Translation

THE COLORS
1. The color of my flag, the color of my flag,
   the color of my flag, red, white, and blue.
2. The color of the desk, the color of the desk,
   the color of the desk, purple and brown.
3. The color of the rainbow, the color of the rainbow,
   the color of the rainbow, pink, green and blue.

8 Colors

Conchita's clues:

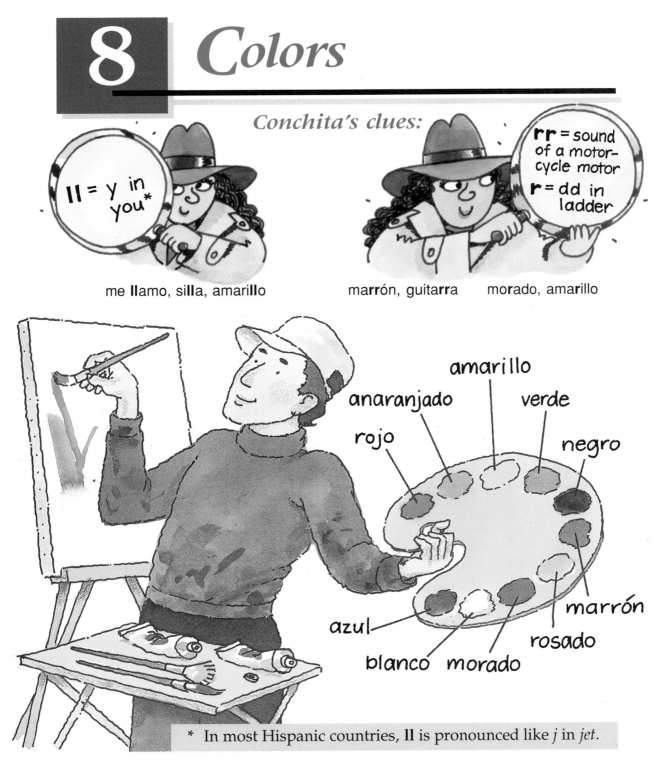

ll = y in you*

me **ll**amo, si**ll**a, amari**ll**o

rr = sound of a motorcycle motor
r = dd in ladder

ma**rr**ón, guita**rr**a   mo**r**ado, ama**r**illo

amarillo

anaranjado   verde

rojo   negro

azul

blanco   morado   rosado   marrón

---

* In most Hispanic countries, **ll** is pronounced like *j* in *jet*.

How many of the Spanish color words can you memorize in one minute? Two minutes? Five? When you feel ready, test yourself:

1. Say as many Spanish color words as you can remember.
2. Write the Spanish color words in the first column of blank lines.
3. Check your work and give yourself one point for each correct answer.
4. Now cover the colors and write the English meanings of the Spanish color words in the second column of blank lines.
5. Check your work and give yourself one point for each correct answer.

WRITE SPANISH WORDS HERE   WRITE ENGLISH WORDS HERE

1. _____   _____

2. _____   _____

3. _____   _____

4. _____   _____

5. _____   _____

6. _____   _____

7. _____   _____

8. _____   _____

9. _____   _____

10. _____   _____

Did you get 20 points? If not, try again with a blank piece of paper.

The following **Actividad** may be done in class or as homework.

ANSWERS TO ACTIVIDAD

1. *rojo*   *red*
2. *anaranjado* *orange*
3. *amarillo*   *yellow*
4. *verde*   *green*
5. *azul*   *blue*
6. *morado*   *purple*
7. *rosado*   *pink*
8. *blanco*   *white*
9. *marrón*   *brown*
10. *negro*   *black*

NOTE TO TEACHERS

This exercise combines objects and colors. Students will receive instructions in how to form feminine adjectives in Section 10, "Talking About Yourself." For now, if students want to describe feminine objects, explain that to form the feminine of adjectives ending in **-o,** they are to change **-o** to **-a.**

Here are pictures of items you have already learned:

Find the objects listed below in the picture above and paint or color them according to the color indicated. Since you have to know the name of the object *and* the color, give yourself two points for each object you color correctly. You can earn a total of twenty points. Perhaps your teacher would like you and a classmate to correct each other's work. Remember, all these words are defined in the vocabulary list at the end of the book:

un pedazo de tiza roja

un lápiz rosado

un cuaderno amarillo

una pluma azul

una pizarra verde

un pupitre morado

un libro anaranjado

un escritorio negro

una puerta marrón

una mesa blanca

You have already seen this map of the world. Color all the countries where Spanish is spoken. Color the countries in each continent according to the colors below:

Europe — **amarillo**

South America — **rojo**

Central America — **azul**

North America — **verde**

Island Countries — **anaranjado**

➡ Have students also name the countries where Spanish is spoken.

➡ As a research project, you may wish students to find the colors of the flags of Spanish-speaking countries. Assign different areas or continents to individual students or groups of students. Students draw, color, and name the colors of the flags. As a class activity, have students collaborate on a color poster of a map and/or the flags of the Spanish-speaking countries.

➡ Here are the colors of the flags of the countries that appear on the map on pages 4 and 5.

Argentina: light blue, white, with yellow sun

Bolivia: red, yellow, green, with emblem

Chile: red, white, blue, with white star

Colombia: yellow, blue, red

Costa Rica: blue, white, red, with emblem

Cuba: blue, white, red, with white star

Dominican Republic: blue, red, white, with emblem

Ecuador: yellow, blue, red, with emblem

El Salvador: blue, white, with emblem

Guatemala: light blue, white, with emblem

Honduras: blue, white, with five blue stars

Mexico: green, white, red, with eagle

Nicaragua: blue, white, with emblem

Panama: red, white, blue, with red and blue star

Paraguay: red, white, blue, with emblem

Peru: red, white, with emblem

Puerto Rico: red, white, blue

Uruguay: blue, white, with sun

Venezuela: yellow, blue, red, with white stars and emblem

➡ You may wish students to research additional information about Spanish-speaking countries: capital, population, currency, important industries and agricultural products, and so on.

NOTE TO TEACHERS

➡ *Conchita's clue:* Model pronunciation of **ñ** sound for students.

➡ At this point, have students learn definite articles. Having previously learned **un** and **una** and the concept of gender, the addition of **el** and **la** follows logically.

➡ Use picture dictation for additional reinforcement. Have students draw the part of the body they hear.

➡ A bingo game can easily be adapted as a listening comprehension activity for parts of the body. Follow instructions for a similar activity on page 36.

9 The Body

Conchita's clue:

ñ = ny in canyon

español, señor, señorita

la cabeza

el ojo

la nariz

la boca

la mano

la oreja

el brazo

la pierna

el pie

When you want to talk about yourself in Spanish, you will need to know the names of the parts of the body. How many names can you remember without having to look at the book?

You have already learned that the masculine article **un** and the feminine article **una** mean *a, an*. Now let's learn how to express English *the*. Did you notice the words **el** and **la** before all of the nouns? To say *the*, Spanish uses **el** before masculine nouns and **la** before feminine nouns.

Fill in the names of the parts of the body:

Choose a partner. Point to each other's hand, foot, and so on, and ask, **"¿Qué es?"** Answer, **"Es una mano." "Es un pie."** And so on.

ANSWERS TO ACTIVIDAD

head	**la cabeza**	eye	**el ojo**
ear	**la oreja**	nose	**la nariz**
mouth	**la boca**	hand	**la mano**
arm	**el brazo**	foot	**el pie**
leg	**la pierna**		

NOTE TO TEACHERS

➡ Model the second **Actividad** with a student in front of the class.

➡ Here is a song that students will enjoy to practice the parts of the body. As students sing, have them point to the part of the body mentioned and make gestures to accompany the verbs.

El cuerpo

1. La ca - be - za, la ca - be - za, la ca - be - za es pa - ra pen - sar.

2. Los ojos, los ojos, los ojos son para ver.
3. Las orejas, las orejas, las orejas para escuchar.
4. La nariz, la nariz, la nariz es para oler.
5. La boca, la boca, la boca es para hablar.
6. Las piernas, las piernas, las piernas para caminar.
7. Los brazos, los brazos, los brazos para abrazar.

Translation
1. *The head, the head, the head is for thinking.*
2. *The eyes, the eyes, the eyes are for seeing.*
3. *The ears, the ears, the ears for listening.*
4. *The nose, the nose, the nose is for smelling.*

THE BODY
5. *The mouth, the mouth, the mouth is for speaking.*
6. *The legs, the legs, the legs for walking.*
7. *The arms, the arms, the arms for hugging.*

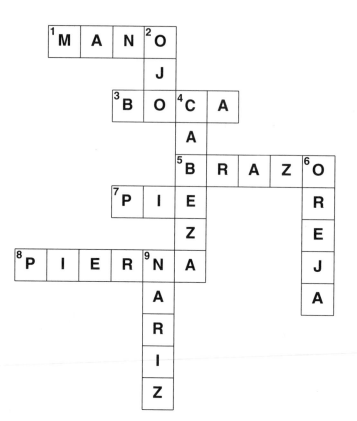

Simón dice: One row of students plays while the rest of the class watches to see who makes a mistake and is eliminated. Have students take turns leading each row. If the leader says, **"Simón dice: la boca,"** students should point to their mouth or make it move. If the leader simply says, **"la boca,"** students remain still. When all rows have played, the winner of each row plays the final round in front of the class.

Complete this crossword puzzle with the
Spanish names of the parts of the body:

Across

Down

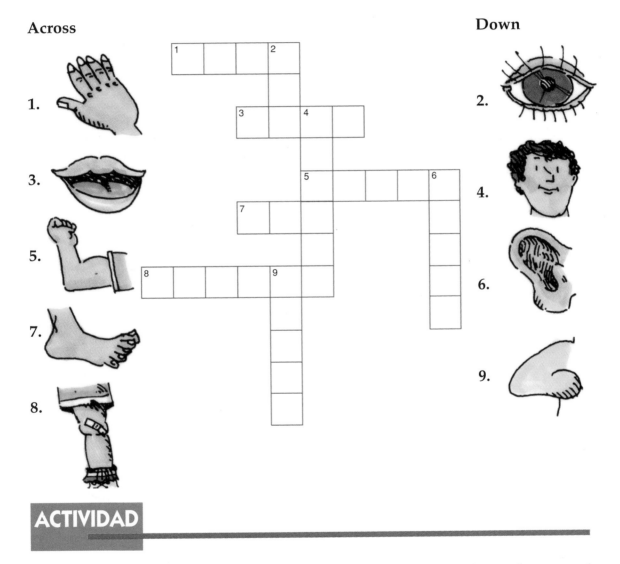

1.

2.

3.

4.

5.

6.

7.

8.

9.

"Simón dice" means *"Simon says."* Move or point to that part of
the body Simon refers to only if you hear the words **"Simón dice."**
If you do not hear the words **"Simón dice,"** don't move at all.

Rincón cultural

Some Interesting Manners and Customs

People of Spanish heritage tend to be very affectionate with family and friends and warm when meeting new people. They readily express their feelings and have more physical contact than Americans. It is common practice for women friends as well as friends of the opposite sex to kiss each other when meeting and again when parting. Men generally greet with a handshake, a pat on the back, and occasionally an embrace. Unlike most Americans, who put a high premium on personal space and privacy, Hispanics enjoy being physically close with their friends. It is not unusual to touch a friend's arm, hand, or leg during conversation, to walk arm in arm, and for younger female friends to hold hands.

In the United States, a formal invitation to dinner is usually necessary. In Spain and Spanish America by contrast, friends will often pop in unexpectedly at mealtime and are automatically invited to share the meal.

People from Spanish-speaking countries differ from Americans not only in what they eat but also in when they eat. Breakfast is served between seven and nine o'clock and is usually light, consisting of fritters, toast, coffee with or without milk, or hot chocolate. Lunch, the biggest meal of the day is served between noon and two o'clock. Supper, generally a light meal, is not

Rincón cultural (Supplementary Culture)

➡ In the United States, the basic monetary unit is the dollar, which is also used in Puerto Rico, although they call it **peso.** What kind of money do the other Spanish-speaking countries use? The most common name for currency is **peso,** but not all **pesos** have the same value. It is used in Argentina, Mexico, Cuba, Colombia, Chile, the Dominican Republic, and Uruguay. Other countries have the following currencies:

Bolivia: **peso boliviano**	Panama: **balboa**
Ecuador: **sucre**	Paraguay: **guaraní**
El Salvador and Costa Rica: **colón**	Peru: **sol**
Guatemala: **quetzal**	Spain: **peseta**
Honduras: **lempira**	Venezuela: **bolívar**
Nicaragua: **córdoba**	

➡ Ask students how many Colombian **pesos** they can buy with a dollar. How many **córdobas?** Have them check the foreign-exchange table in the local newspaper for the latest information.

Rincón cultural (Supplementary Culture)

Hispanics customarily shake hands more frequently than Americans when greeting each other. In general, people shake hands every time they meet and every time they part. Unlike the American handshake, which consists of gripping the hand and raising and lowering it several times, the Hispanic handshake consists of a single firm grip of the right hand with the left hand lightly holding the other person's upper arm.

eaten earlier than 7:00 p.m. and often not until nine or ten o'clock at night. At the beginning of a meal, it is customary for everyone at the table to say **"¡Buen provecho!"** (*"Enjoy the meal!"*)

Americans are sometimes puzzled when they observe people from Spanish-speaking countries during mealtime because they hold the fork in the left hand and the knife in the right, keeping them this way throughout the meal, even after cutting their food. The knife is not put down while eating and the fork does not change hands.

Would you be confused if you opened a Spanish television guide and saw listed programs starting at 18:00, 22:00, or 00:30 o'clock? Spanish-speaking countries use the 24-hour system for official time — schedules for planes, trains, radio and television programs, movies, sports events, and so on. With this system, they avoid confusion as well as the need to use a.m. or p.m.

CONVENTIONAL TIME	OFFICIAL TIME
8:00 a.m.	08,00 **(a las ocho)**
noon	12,00 **(a las doce)**
2:00 p.m.	14,00 **(a las catorce)**
6 p.m.	18,00 **(a las diez y ocho)**
midnight	24,00 **(a las veinte y cuatro)**
12:15 a.m.	00,15 **(a las zero y quince)**

To calculate official time, add 12 to the conventional time for the hours between noon and midnight:

8:00 a.m.	08,00
8:00 p.m.	20,00

10 Talking About Yourself

An adjective describes a person or thing. In the sentence "The beautiful girl is happy," *beautiful* and *happy* are adjectives that describe *girl*. Many adjectives are easy to remember if you think of them in pairs:

delgado   **gordo**   **inteligente**   **tonto**

triste   **alegre**   **pequeño**   **grande**

guapo   **feo**   **fuerte**   **débil**

➡ Model pronunciation of adjectives or have students listen to the cassette, allowing time for repetition. To teach adjectives, have a student mime adjectives while the class tries to guess the adjective being acted out.

➡ Here is a song students will enjoy to practice adjectives with. Other adjectives and classroom objects may be substituted for additional practice.

Adjetivos

1. Gua - po, gua - po, gua - po, gua - po, es muy gua - po el mu - cha - chi - to.

2. Guapa, guapa, guapa, guapa, es muy guapa la profesora.
3. Feo, feo, feo, feo, es muy feo el escritorio.
4. Fea, fea, fea, fea, es muy fea la silla negra.
5. Triste, triste, triste, triste, es muy triste la señorita.
6. Grande, grande, grande, grande, es muy grande el libro verde.
7. Fuerte, fuerte, fuerte, fuerte, es muy fuerte el estudiante.

Translation

ADJECTIVES

1. *Handsome, handsome, handsome, handsome, he's a very handsome little boy.*
2. *Beautiful, beautiful, beautiful, beautiful, she's a very beautiful teacher.*
3. *Ugly, ugly, ugly, ugly, it's a very ugly desk.*
4. *Ugly, ugly, ugly, ugly, it's a very ugly black chair.*
5. *Sad, sad, sad, sad, she's a very sad young woman.*
6. *Big, big, big, big, it's a very big green book.*
7. *Strong, strong, strong, strong, he's a very strong student.*

ANSWERS TO ACTIVIDAD

1. *guapo*   2. *feo*   3. *triste*

4. *alegre*   5. *fuerte*   6. *débil*

7. *delgado*   8. *gordo*   9. *pequeño*

10. *grande*   11. *inteligente*   12. *tonto*

NOTE TO TEACHERS

➡ When students have completed the **Actividad**, you may ask them to name as well as describe the objects illustrated. Note: All adjectives are masculine in gender or invariable.

+ **El lápiz guapo.**   **El lápiz feo.**

+ **El papel triste.**   **El papel alegre.**

+ **La silla fuerte.**   **La silla débil.**

+ **El libro delgado.**   **El libro gordo.**

+ **El pupitre pequeño.**   **El pupitre grande.**

+ **El cuaderno inteligente.**   **El cuaderno tonto.**

➡ You may wish to introduce **es** *(is)* at this point and have students describe the objects using complete sentences.

+ **El libro es delgado.**

+ **El cuaderno es tonto.** And so on.

Cover page 52 with a sheet of paper and write the Spanish adjectives that describe the objects you see:

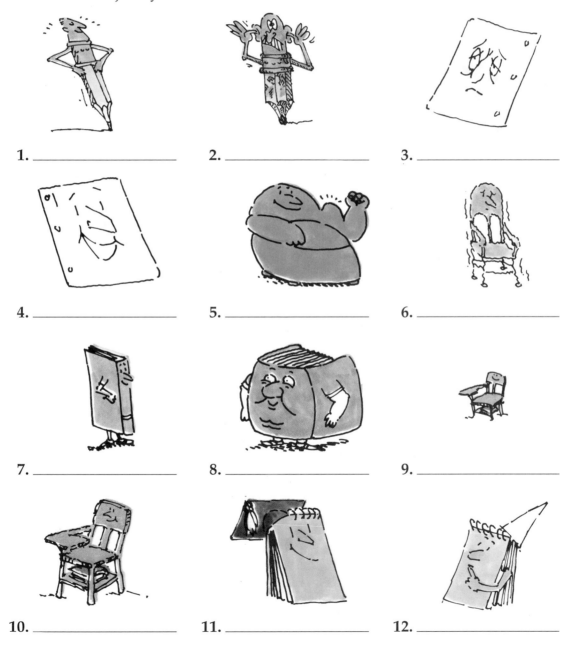

1. _____

2. _____

3. _____

4. _____

5. _____

6. _____

7. _____

8. _____

9. _____

10. _____

11. _____

12. _____

* Note that Spanish speakers commonly omit **yo** and **tú** before the verb.

NOTE TO TEACHERS

➡ Before students are asked to read **Diálogo** 3 for meaning, have them look at the characters and guess what Elisa and Jaime may be feeling and saying to each other in each illustration.

➡ Next, model pronunciation either by reading aloud or by playing the cassette while students read the dialog.

➡ Now have students read the dialog for meaning. Refer them to the vocabulary list at the end of the book for words and phrases they do not understand.

➡ Explain that both **yo estoy** and **yo soy** mean *I am*, and **tú estás** and **tú eres** mean *you are*. Point out that **por qué** means *why* and **porque** means *because*.

NOTE TO TEACHERS *(Optional Diálogo 4, page 55)*

➡ **Diálogo** 4 is provided for teachers who wish to introduce **usted** and other formal expressions. You may reproduce it for your students. **Diálogo** 4 may be presented at the end of Section 10, "Talking About Yourself."

➡ Before students are asked to read **Diálogo** 4 for meaning, have them scan the dialog for familiar words and expressions and guess the general content of the conversation.

➡ Next, model pronunciation either by reading aloud or by playing the cassette while students read the dialog.

➡ Now have students close their books. Read short segments for students to repeat. Use the "backward buildup" approach.

➡ Ask questions:

- ◆ How do Elisa and Jaime greet each other in the evening?
- ◆ How does Elisa ask Jaime, "Who is that?"
- ◆ What is the woman's profession?
- ◆ How does Elisa ask the Spanish teacher her name?
- ◆ How does Mrs. Rivera ask Elisa her name?
- ◆ How do the Spanish say, "His name is ____"?
- ◆ How does Jaime ask Mrs. Rivera how she is?
- ◆ How does she respond?

➡ Point out the difference between formal and informal expressions:

¿Cómo se llama usted?	¿Cómo te llamas tú?
Usted es . . .	Tú eres . . .
¿Cómo está usted?	¿Cómo estás tú?

➡ New vocabulary and expressions:

Buenas noches.	*Good evening.*
¿Quién es?	*Who is it?*
Es la profesora de español.	*It's the Spanish teacher.*
¿Cómo se llama (usted)?	*What's your name? (formal)*
¿Cómo te llamas (tú)?	*What's your name? (informal)*
¿Cómo se llama (ella)?	*What's her name?*
No sé.	*I don't know.*
Él (Ella) se llama . . .	*His (Her) name is . . .*
Usted es la profesora de español.	*You are the Spanish teacher. (formal)*
¿Verdad?	*Right? Isn't that so?*
¿Cómo está (usted)?	*How are you? (formal)*
¿Cómo estás (tú)?	*How are you? (informal)*

Diálogo 4 *(Optional)*

Buenas noches

Elisa and Jaime meet at an international school fair organized by the foreign language department of their school. It is 7:00 P.M.

Elisa:	**Buenas noches, Jaime.**
Jaime:	**Buenas noches, Elisa.**

Elisa points to a woman.

Elisa:	**¿Quién es?**
Jaime:	**Es la profesora de español.**
Elisa:	**¿Cómo se llama ella?**
Jaime:	**No sé.**

Elisa walks toward the Spanish teacher.

Elisa:	**Buenas noches, señora. ¿Usted es la profesora de español, verdad?**
Mrs. Rivera:	**Sí. ¿Cómo te llamas?**
Elisa:	**Me llamo Elisa. ¿Y usted, cómo se llama?**
Mrs. Rivera:	**Yo me llamo Julia Rivera.**

Elisa and Mrs. Rivera shake hands.

Elisa:	**Mucho gusto, señora Rivera.**
Mrs. Rivera:	**Mucho gusto, Elisa.**

Elisa gestures to Jaime to join them.

Elisa:	**Él se llama Jaime.**
Mrs. Rivera:	**Buenas noches, Jaime. Me llamo Julia Rivera.**
Jaime:	**Mucho gusto, señora Rivera. ¿Cómo está usted?**
Mrs. Rivera:	**Muy bien, gracias.**

In Dialog 3, you may have noticed that Spanish has two ways of saying *I am*: **yo estoy** and **yo soy**. Let's compare the difference between these two forms:

estoy is used to describe how you feel at the moment you are speaking:

Yo estoy alegre. *I am happy.*

Yo estoy triste. *I am sad.*

soy is used to describe what kind of person you are all the time:

Yo soy inteligente. *I am intelligent.*

Yo soy guapo. *I am good-looking.*

Look at these pictures. Can you explain why the girl uses **yo estoy** and the boy uses **yo soy**?

One more point. When you want to say *you are*, choose between **tú estás** and **tú eres**:

Tú estás alegre.   Tú eres inteligente.

To say *he is* choose between **él está** and **él es**; and to say *she is* choose between **ella está** and **ella es**.

Él / Ella está triste.   Él / Ella es fuerte.

➡ Have class repeat, **"Estoy triste."** Then say, **"alegre."** The class repeats, **"Estoy alegre."**

➡ Follow the same procedure with **tú estás.**

➡ Present **el muchacho está, la muchacha está, él está,** and **ella está.** Practice these three forms of **estar** until the class has mastered them.

➡ Have class repeat, **"Soy inteligente."** Then say, **"fuerte."** The class is to repeat, **"Soy fuerte."** (**Inteligente, fuerte, débil,** and **grande** have similar masculine and feminine forms. Limit yourself to these adjectives until after the next section.)

➡ Follow the same procedure with **tú eres, el muchacho es, la muchacha es, él es,** and **ella es.** Practice these three forms of **ser** until the class has mastered them.

➡ Explain the difference between the use of **ser** and **estar.**

◆ Point out that **estar** is used to describe a physical or emotional condition that can change quickly. You may wish to give the following example:

Tú estás alegre. (Your mother tells you to go clean your room and then **Tú estás triste.**)

◆ Continue to explain that to express a permanent characteristic or one that cannot change quickly, they are to use **ser.** Give students the following example:

El muchacho es pequeño. (No matter how much spinach the boy eats, he will not grow overnight.)

Note to Teachers

Ask students why they chose **estar** or **ser** for each illustration.

ANSWERS TO ACTIVIDAD

1. *Yo soy inteligente.*

2. *Tú eres tonto.*

3. *El muchacho (Él) es grande.*

4. *La muchacha (Ella) está alegre.*

Now it's your turn. Can you complete what the young people in these pictures are saying? Use a form of **ser** or **estar** followed by an adjective:

1.

2.

3.

4.

Let's learn some more about adjectives. Look at the adjectives on the left that could describe a boy. Compare them with the adjectives on the right that could describe a girl:

delgado	delgada
gordo	gorda
tonto	tonta
guapo	guapa
feo	fea
pequeño	pequeña

Spanish adjectives, like nouns, have a gender. A feminine adjective is used to describe a feminine noun and a masculine adjective is used to describe a masculine noun. Which letter do we change in the masculine adjective to get the feminine?

ACTIVIDAD

Use as many of the adjectives above to describe these animals:

_____   _____

_____   _____

_____   _____

_____   _____

NOTE TO TEACHERS

➡ Model pronunciation of feminine and masculine adjectives for students, allowing time for repetition.

➡ Remind students that they have already learned the rule to form the feminine of adjectives: Adjectives ending in **-o** change the **-o** to **-a**. All other adjectives remain unchanged.

➡ You may wish to use picture dictation as a listening comprehension activity. Have students first write and then draw what they hear, for example: **La muchacha está alegre. El muchacho es grande. La profesora es gorda. El profesor es pequeño.** Have students check and correct each other's pictures. You may wish to create a composite poster of students' drawings for display in the classroom.

➡ Have students respond to questions about yourself, themselves, and each other. Accompany questions with body language and mime and elicit the same from students whenever appropriate. Here are some sample questions:

◆ Ask students about yourself:

TEACHER	STUDENT
¿Yo soy tonto(a)?	**No, tú eres inteligente.**
¿Yo soy guapo(a)?	**Sí, tú eres guapo(a).**

◆ Ask students about themselves:

TEACHER	STUDENT
¿Tú eres feo(a)?	**No, yo soy guapo(a).**
¿Tú eres gordo(a)?	**No, yo soy delgado(a).**

◆ Ask one student while pointing to another:

TEACHER	STUDENT
¿Él es grande?	**No, él es pequeño.**
¿Ella es tonta?	**No, ella es inteligente.**

ANSWERS TO ACTIVIDAD

El dinosaurio	La rata
guapo	*fea*
tonto	*tonta*
alegre	*triste*
pequeño	*pequeña*

➡ Model pronunciation for students, repeating and filling in missing words.

ANSWERS TO ACTIVIDAD

1. La muchacha está **triste.**

   El profesor está **triste** también.

2. El muchacho es **débil.**

   La muchacha es **débil** también.

3. ¡El muchacho es **fuerte**!

   ¡No, la muchacha es **fuerte**!

NOTE TO TEACHERS

➡ For additional practice, have students find and describe magazine pictures of movie and television stars, athletes, cartoon characters, and so on. Students may also enjoy bringing in photographs of family members or friends. Have students describe the people in their pictures to their classmates, for example:

> **Goofy es tonto. / Él es tonto.**
> **Michael Jordan es grande. / Él es grande.**
> **Roseanne es gorda. / Ella es gorda.**

You may also wish students to name the people in their pictures before describing them:

> **Él se llama Superman. Superman es fuerte.**
> **Ella se llama Conchita. Ella es inteligente.**

You have already learned that changing the final **o** of a Spanish adjective to **a** gives you the feminine form. Now let's learn about the feminine forms of other adjectives.

Adjectives that do not end in **o** — like **alegre, triste, inteligente, fuerte, grande,** and **débil** — do not change in the feminine. Isn't that easy?

Let's practice these adjectives by filling in the blanks with the adjective that describes the people in the pictures:

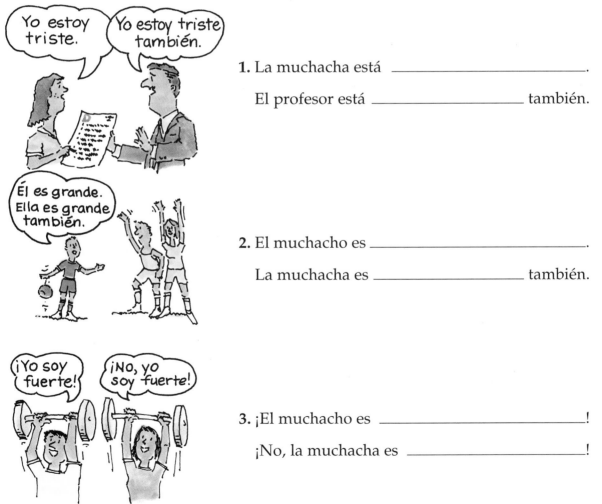

1. La muchacha está _____.

   El profesor está _____ también.

2. El muchacho es _____.

   La muchacha es _____ también.

3. ¡El muchacho es _____!

   ¡No, la muchacha es _____!

1. How many of the boys in this basketball team can you describe? Write the adjective that best describes each player next to his number in the column of blank lines:

MUCHACHOS

1	_____
2	_____
3	_____
4	_____
5	_____
6	_____
7	_____
8	_____
9	_____
10	_____

ANSWERS TO ACTIVIDAD

MUCHACHOS

1	*guapo*
2	*alegre*
3	*grande*
4	*débil*
5	*gordo*
6	*fuerte*
7	*triste*
8	*delgado*
9	*pequeño*
10	*inteligente*

ANSWERS TO ACTIVIDAD

MUCHACHAS

1   *gorda*

2   *alegre*

3   *inteligente*

4   *triste*

5   *pequeña*

6   *delgada*

7   *fuerte*

8   *grande*

9   *débil*

10   *guapa*

2. How would you change the adjectives to describe each player of the opposing girls' team? Write the adjective that best describes each player next to her number in the column of blank lines:

MUCHACHAS

1 _____

2 _____

3 _____

4 _____

5 _____

6 _____

7 _____

8 _____

9 _____

10 _____

Your teacher will now divide you into small groups to practice describing yourself and one another.

Play charades with the adjectives you have learned. Your teacher will divide the class into teams, and a member from one team will stand in front of the class and act out the various ways he or she would look if sad, intelligent, fat, and so on.

Rincón cultural

Los deportes (Sports)

In Spain and Spanish America, soccer **(fútbol)** is a passion bordering on obsession. Most large and small cities have their own teams. Many different types of soccer teams are popular: neighborhood teams, company teams, soccer club teams, as well as professional teams. National games are very important and the competition is fierce. International soccer competitions are occasions for great patriotic enthusiasm, and soccer teams are revered as national symbols. In almost every park and empty lot in every town, boys of all ages can be seen playing soccer and dreaming of becoming the next international soccer star.

➡ Have students in groups of three or four practice describing one another. Demonstrate with two or three students in front of the class.

¡Yo soy fuerte! ¡Tú eres fuerte también!

No, yo soy débil. Pero yo soy inteligente.

¿Tú estás triste?

No, yo estoy alegre. ¡Y yo soy muy guapo(a) también!

➡ You may wish to use the following writing activity to review structures and vocabulary learned in this section:

◆ Make a copy of **Diálogo** 3 on pages 54 and 55 and whiten out the text in the bubbles.

◆ Divide the students into pairs and distribute a dialog to each student.

◆ Have partners create a dialog to be inserted in the empty bubbles. Refer students to the vocabulary list at the end of the book for words and phrases they may need.

◆ Circulate among students, advising, correcting, and answering questions.

◆ When dialogs have been completed and corrected, have students memorize them and dramatize them for the class.

Rincón cultural (Supplementary Culture)

➡ Bullfighting (**corrida de toros**) is prohibited in some Spanish-speaking countries, but it is still popular in Spain, Mexico, Peru, Colombia, and Venezuela. Bullfights date back to the 1700s when Spain built its first bullring. Bullfighting may have roots in ancient Rome where gladiators fought wild animals for public entertainment. The **corridas** are held on Sunday afternoons, and each **corrida** lasts approximately twenty minutes. When a bullfighter shows good technique, is graceful, and exposes himself to great danger, spectators yell "¡Olé!" When they are disappointed, they whistle loudly. In spite of its popularity, many oppose bullfighting as a cruel sport and would like to see it abolished everywhere.

Answers will vary.

What is less known is that other sports, like baseball, are also becoming more and more popular in many Hispanic countries. In the Caribbean, in Cuba, the Dominican Republic, Puerto Rico, Mexico, Nicaragua, and Venezuela, baseball is as important or even more important than soccer. Many famous major league baseball players in the United States have come from Cuba, the Dominican Republic, and Puerto Rico.

Cycling is very important in Spain, Colombia, Mexico, Cuba, Chile, and Costa Rica. Each country has its national race once a year that lasts a couple of weeks. The winner is a national hero.

There is also a lesser known, very ancient sport, **jai-alai**, which has its origins in the Basque region of Spain. It's probably the fastest game in the world. Played with a hard ball and a wicker basket strapped to the wrist on a court with high walls, **jai-alai** resembles handball, except for the basket. This sport is popular in Spain, Cuba, Mexico, and Venezuela, as well as in Florida and Connecticut.

Spain as well as some Spanish-American countries, especially Mexico and Colombia, are also known for bullfighting (**corridas de toro**).

1. Which sports are most popular in America? _____

_____

2. Would you be interested in seeing a bullfight? _____

_____

11 Recycling Spanish

Your teacher will now give you time to use your Spanish. Think of all you have learned!

- You can say your name!
- You can count and do math!
- You can name the days of the week and the months of the year!

- You can name objects in the classroom with their colors!
- You can describe yourself and others and point out parts of the body!

When someone asks if you speak Spanish: **¿Hablas español?**, now you can answer: **¡Sí, hablo español!**

ACTIVIDAD

Fill in the boxes with the Spanish meanings and you will find a mystery word in the longest vertical column. Write the mystery word in Spanish and English in the blanks provided:

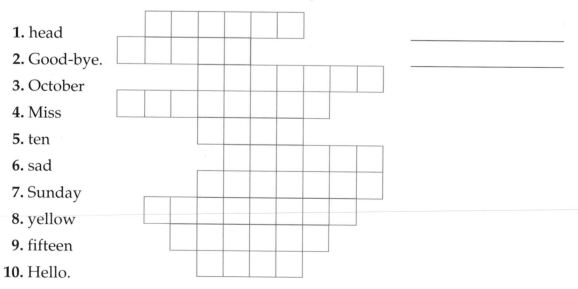

1. head
2. Good-bye.
3. October
4. Miss
5. ten
6. sad
7. Sunday
8. yellow
9. fifteen
10. Hello.

NOTE TO TEACHERS

➡ As a culminating activity, give students the opportunity to make an oral presentation on a cultural topic studied. You may wish to divide the class into small groups, with each student contributing to the research of the topic. The group then chooses a representative to speak in front the class.

➡ Now would be a good time to teach **¿Hablas español?** and **Hablo español.** Give students a chance both to ask and answer the question.

Mystery word: *escritorio*
              teacher's desk

1.		C	A	B	E	Z	A		
2.	A	D	I	O	S				
3.				O	C	T	U	B	R	E
4.	S	E	N	O	R	I	T	A	
5.				D	I	E	Z		
6.					T	R	I	S	T	E
7.				D	O	M	I	N	G	O
8.		A	M	A	R	I	L	L	O
9.			Q	U	I	N	C	E	
10.				H	O	L	A		

ANSWERS TO ACTIVIDAD *(Colors will vary.)*

1. *la cabeza*

2. *la boca*

3. *el ojo*

4. *la oreja*

5. *la nariz*

6. *la mano*

7. *la pierna*

8. *el pie*

9. *el brazo*

NOTE TO TEACHERS

➡ Have students correct each other's work as you circulate among the class, checking students' answers.

➡ For additional speaking practice of vocabulary and the verb **ser,** you may wish to have students show their colored monster picture to the class and describe its colors in complete sentences. Students point to a part of the body and say, for example, **"La nariz es roja."**

Model a masculine and a feminine example before students begin:
   El pie es negro.
   La cabeza es verde.

Have the class play the role of teacher and correct classmates' errors in Spanish.

Colors: What would this funny monster look like if you could color the parts of its body? Write the names of the parts of the body and colors you would choose in the blanks below. Then color the parts of the body in the picture:

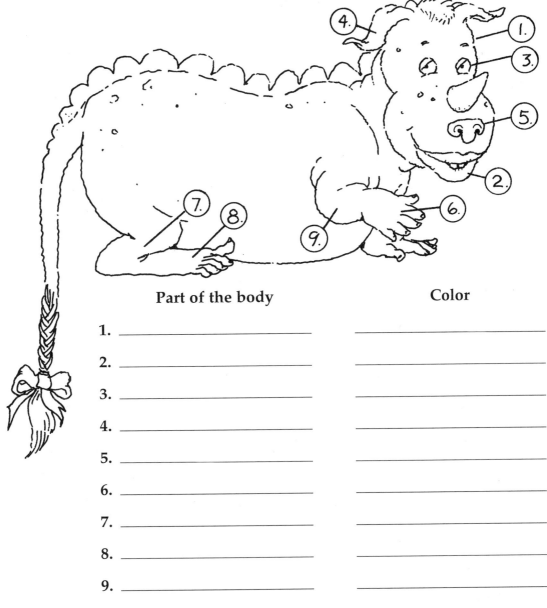

Part of the body	Color
1. _____	_____
2. _____	_____
3. _____	_____
4. _____	_____
5. _____	_____
6. _____	_____
7. _____	_____
8. _____	_____
9. _____	_____

Can you complete these dialogs or express the following ideas in Spanish?

1. You overhear the conversation of these two people, who are meeting for the first time. Complete the dialog:

Sample Answers to Actividad

1. Girl: *¡Hola! ¿Cómo te llamas?*

Boy: *¡Hola! Me llamo Jaime, ¿y tú?*

Girl: *Me llamo Elisa. Mucho gusto.*

Boy: *Mucho gusto, Elisa. ¿Cómo estás?*

Girl: *Estoy muy bien. ¿Y tú?*

Boy: *Así, así.*

Sample Answers (continued)

1. Girl: *¿Cómo estás ahora?* or *Adiós Jaime.*

  Boy: *Estoy muy bien ahora. Adiós Elisa.*

2. Peter: *¿Qué es?*

  Brother: *Es un libro.*

  Peter: *¿Qué es?*

  Brother: *¿Es una pluma?*

2. Peter is teaching some Spanish words to his little brother.
Complete the dialog:

3. What do you think these friends are saying to each other?

4. What are the colors of
the Mexican flag?

_____ _____ _____

5. What are the names of these parts of the body?

_____ _____ _____

Sample Answers (continued)

3. Girl: **Muchas gracias.**

    Boy: **De nada.**

4. *verde*   *blanco*   *rojo*

5. *boca*   *pie*   *mano*

ANSWERS TO ACTIVIDAD

6.

ENERO
9 lunes
10 *martes*
11 miércoles
12 *jueves*
13 viernes
14 *sábado*
15 *domingo*

7. *abril*   *agosto*   *diciembre*

8. *débil*   *gorda*   *guapo*

6. What days of the week are missing from this agenda?

7. What month is it?

_____   _____   _____

8. What adjectives describe these people?

_____   _____   _____

Tómbola is played like Bingo, except that our **Tómbola** is played with words. Select Spanish words from categories in the vocabulary list on pages 72 to 74 as directed by your teacher. Write one word across each square at random from the chosen categories.

Your teacher will read the **Tómbola** words in English. If one of the Spanish words on your card matches the English word you hear, mark that square with a small star. When you have five stars in a row, either horizontally, vertically, or diagonally, call out, **"¡Gané!"** *("I won!")*

NOTE TO TEACHERS

➡ Explain that the Spanish game **Tómbola** is the equivalent of bingo.

➡ Model **Gané** *(I won)* for students.

➡ Choose categories of vocabulary you wish students to review. Complete a bingo board with 25 words from the chosen categories and have students take turns reading the words aloud for the class.

➡ Check to see if a word has been spelled correctly before declaring a student a winner.

NOTE TO TEACHERS

➡ As students encountered Spanish-speaking people and their language, they were probably both entertained and impressed by the cultural differences. Now is the time to reinforce respect for Spanish-American culture and foster appreciation for cultural differences.

Sample Answers

➡ You may wish to discuss further how Americans generally greet one another. Ask students how they and their parents greet close family members, relatives, good friends, and acquaintances.

SPANISH	AMERICAN
2. *Friends and relatives greet each other with "Hola" and kisses on both cheeks.*	*Friends and relatives say "Hi" and may kiss women on the cheek.*
3. *Children receive Christmas presents on the day of the Epiphany, January 6.*	*Children receive Christmas presents on December 25.*
4. *People celebrate birthdays as well as name days.*	*People celebrate birthdays.*
5. *The word "family" includes parents, children, grandparents, aunts, uncles, and cousins.*	*The word "family" usually means parents and children.*
6. *Soccer is the most popular sport.*	*Football, basketball, baseball, and hockey are the most popular sports.*

Rincón cultural

¡Vivan las diferencias! (Hurrah for the differences!)

Now that you have learned quite a bit about the Spanish language and about the Spanish-speaking world and its people, can you list the differences that impressed you most between Hispanic and American people. Jog your memory by looking over cultural pages 16–17, 25, 34–35, 42, 50–51, and 62–63.

An example is given to get you started:

SPANISH	AMERICAN
1. *Each person uses the father's last name plus the mother's maiden name.*	*Only one family name is used: the father's last name.*
2.	
3.	
4.	
5.	
6.	

Vocabulary

Numbers

uno	1
dos	2
tres	3
cuatro	4
cinco	5
seis	6
siete	7
ocho	8
nueve	9
diez	10
once	11
doce	12
trece	13
catorce	14
quince	15
diez y seis	16
diez y siete	17
diez y ocho	18
diez y nueve	19
veinte	20
veinte y uno	21
veinte y dos	22
veinte y tres	23
veinte y cuatro	24
veinte y cinco	25
veinte y seis	26
veinte y siete	27
veinte y ocho	28
veinte y nueve	29
treinta	30
treinta y uno	31
treinta y dos	32
treinta y tres	33
treinta y cuatro	34
treinta y cinco	35
treinta y seis	36
treinta y siete	37
treinta y ocho	38
treinta y nueve	39
cuarenta	40

Arithmetic

¿Cuántos?	How many?
y	plus
menos	minus
son	are, equal

Days of the week

lunes	Monday
martes	Tuesday
miércoles	Wednesday
jueves	Thursday
viernes	Friday
sábado	Saturday
domingo	Sunday

Months of the year

enero	January
febrero	February
marzo	March
abril	April
mayo	May
junio	June
julio	July
agosto	August
septiembre	September
octubre	October
noviembre	November
diciembre	December

The Classroom

un cuaderno	a notebook
un escritorio	a teacher's desk
un(a) estudiante	a student
una hoja de papel	a piece of paper
un lápiz	a pencil
un libro	a book
una mesa	a table
una muchacha	a girl
un muchacho	a boy
una pizarra	a chalkboard
una pluma	a pen
un profesor	a male teacher
una profesora	a female teacher
una puerta	a door

un pupitre	a student's desk
un pedazo de tiza	a piece of chalk
un profesor	a male teacher
una profesora	a female teacher
una silla	a chair
una ventana	a window

Colors

amarillo, amarilla	yellow
anaranjado, anaranjada	orange
azul	blue
blanco, blanca	white
morado, morada	purple
marrón	brown
negro, negra	black
rojo, roja	red
rosado, rosada	pink
verde	green

The Body

la boca	the mouth
el brazo	the arm
la cabeza	the head
la mano	the hand
la nariz	the nose
el ojo	the eye
la oreja	the ear
el pie	the foot
la pierna	the leg

Adjectives

alegre	happy
débil	weak
delgado, delgada	thin
feo, fea	ugly
fuerte	strong
gordo, gorda	fat
grande	tall, big
guapo, guapa	beautiful, handsome
inteligente	intelligent
pequeño, pequeña	small, short
tonto, tonta	stupid
triste	sad

Expressions and phrases

Buenos días.	Good morning.
Adiós.	Good-bye.
¡Hola!	Hello! / Hi!
¿Cómo te llamas?	What's your name?
Me llamo . . .	My name is . . .
¿Y tú?	And you?
Mucho gusto.	Pleased to meet you.
El gusto es mío.	The pleasure is mine.
¿Cómo estás?	How are you?
Estoy muy bien.	I am very well.
Así, así.	So, so.
¿Qué es?	What is it?
¿Cuántos?	How many?
Es un (una) . . .	It is a . . .
Para ti.	For you.

Gracias.	Thank you.
Muchas gracias.	Thank you very much.
De nada.	You're welcome.
Yo estoy . . .	I am . . .
Tú estás . . .	You are . . .
Ella / Él está . . .	She / He is . . .
La muchacha está . . .	The girl is . . .
El muchacho está . . .	The boy is . . .
Yo soy . . .	I am . . .
Tú eres . . .	You are . . .
Ella / Él es . . .	She / He is . . .
La muchacha es . . .	The girl is . . .
El muchacho es . . .	The boy is . . .
Hoy es . . .	Today is . . .
Lo siento.	I'm sorry.
Por favor.	Please.
¿Por qué?	Why?
porque	because
y	and
muy	very
ahora	now
también	also
Sí.	Yes.
No.	No.
señor	Mister, sir
señora	Mrs., madame
señorita	Miss
Rincón cultural	Cultural corner